CHALLENGES FOR RELIGIOUS EDUCATION

Major social changes, especially as a result of the more multicultural nature of society, have raised important issues about the teaching of religion and the rational basis of different religious faiths. *Challenges for Religious Education* addresses and critically examines these changes and asks where religious education and Faith Schools fit within secular society and indeed whether there is still a place for them at all.

Analysing what religious education could look like if it were considered from a wider 'world views' perspective that doesn't focus on a particular set of religious beliefs, this book considers the 'reasonableness' of holding a faith and therefore in teaching it; the ongoing tensions between faith and reason; arguments for and against the study of religious education; whether modern secular thought is itself an ideology; and the philosophical standpoints on the relationship between faith and reason.

Linking faith and reason with the issue of whether religious education is truly necessary in a modern world, *Challenges for Religious Education* is a crucial read for anyone interested in the future of religious education teaching in a secular society.

Richard Pring is Emeritus Professor of Education, and formerly Director of the Department of Educational Studies, University of Oxford, UK. His recent and relevant books include *The Future of Publicly Funded Faith Schools* (2018) and *Thinking Philosophically about Education* (2018) both published by Routledge.

CHALLENGES FOR RELIGIOUS EDUCATION

Is There a Disconnect Between Faith and Reason?

Richard Pring

LONDON AND NEW YORK

First published 2020
by Routledge
2 Park Square, Milton Park, Abingdon, Oxon, OX14 4RN

and by Routledge
52 Vanderbilt Avenue, New York, NY 10017

Routledge is an imprint of the Taylor & Francis Group, an informa business

© 2020 Richard Pring

The right of Richard Pring to be identified as author of this work has been asserted by him in accordance with sections 77 and 78 of the Copyright, Designs and Patents Act 1988.

All rights reserved. No part of this book may be reprinted or reproduced or utilised in any form or by any electronic, mechanical, or other means, now known or hereafter invented, including photocopying and recording, or in any information storage or retrieval system, without permission in writing from the publishers.

Trademark notice: Product or corporate names may be trademarks or registered trademarks, and are used only for identification and explanation without intent to infringe.

British Library Cataloguing-in-Publication Data
A catalogue record for this book is available from the British Library

Library of Congress Cataloging-in-Publication Data
A catalog record for this book has been requested

ISBN: 978-0-367-27906-6 (hbk)
ISBN: 978-0-367-27907-3 (pbk)
ISBN: 978-0-429-29865-3 (ebk)

Typeset in Bembo
by Apex CoVantage, LLC

To Faye, Helen, Katherine and Sally

CONTENTS

Introduction	1
1 Teaching religious education: changing conceptions of RE	3
2 Faith: meaning and reasonableness	20
3 Belief in God: knowledge, evidence and assent	33
4 Understanding the nature of God	49
5 The moral dimension: has God got a place within it?	58
6 Spiritual development	69
7 Coping with doubt – and the problem of evil	77
8 Surviving the secular age?	88
9 The challenges for religious education	101
10 Indoctrination?	118
Name Index	*121*
Subject Index	*123*

INTRODUCTION

In a book recently published by Routledge (*The Future of Publicly Funded Faith Schools*), I pointed to the increasing and often hostile objections to the continuation of financial support for Faith Schools within the State system of education. It is now commonly argued that in a secular society there is need for a secular system of education, one which does not discriminate in admissions to state-funded schools on the basis of a religious faith. Within a secular system there would doubtless be a place for some form of religious education, but not one which is based on a particular set of religious beliefs. Indeed, the 2017 Commission on Religious Education for England and Wales recommended that the subject should be renamed as 'Religion and World Views', enabling young people, in their preparation for life in modern society, to have knowledge about religious and non-religious world views but without commitment to (or encouragement to be committed to) any one of them.

Such a view, though gradually emerging in practice in Britain over several decades, is radically different from the 19th-century beginning of the national system of education when a Christian culture was taken for granted and religious teaching was based on Christian foundations.

But many of the issues underpinning this cultural shift are by no means peculiar to Britain, in particular that of promoting 'a faith' within an educational context where a main purpose of such a context is, or should be, to develop rationality in its different forms. Therefore, we have seen within the increasingly more secular cultures vigorous debates on the nature and practice of religious education in schools – but also, on the other hand, and partly in response to such secular cultures, the determination of particular religious bodies to preserve within their respective state-financed schools a faith-based approach to education and to the religious education curriculum.

Therefore, although the immediate focus of this book is upon England and Wales, but with special reference to Ireland because of the debate there on the nature and practice of religious education in schools, the central philosophical issues raised are of wider international significance concerning the 'reasonableness' in holding a religious faith, the reasonableness therefore in teaching it, and the appropriateness of the 'religious formation' within it, should that be what the parents wish, even though within the non-religious State systems.

In this regard, special reference will be made, particularly in Chapter 1, to the emerging approach to Faith Schools in Ireland and to the teaching of religious education there, as an increasingly secularist context indicates a break from a system shaped by religious ethos and foundations. Reference will also be made throughout, but particularly in Chapter 8, to the alternative arguments for a distinctively secular education as developed, for example, by Emile Durkheim, and which prevails in France.

The changes in the social context, especially as a result of immigration and the more multicultural nature of society, raise important issues about the teaching of religion and the rational basis of different religious faiths. In that respect the differences, but at the same time the connections, between the major Abrahamic religious faiths (Christianity, Islam and Judaism) cannot be ignored in seeking a way forward for religious education and formation.

A key issue, therefore, as with the teaching of any content in an educational context, must concern the nature of religion as a body of knowledge, thereby having truth claims and rational foundations. To what extent are such claims, and the way of life and human formation which accompany them, defensible within an educational context?

The answer requires a deeper and more systematic account of the relationship between 'faith' and 'reason', drawing upon a long and too-often ignored tradition of philosophical examination of the issues. Frequently a more philosophical answer to such a question has not been forthcoming or directed at those who, unaware of such traditions, too easily dismiss such claims in favour of a purely secular understanding of the universe and thereby of the educational system in which education is to take place.

It is therefore the aim of this book to go more deeply into this debate – that is, to argue for the teaching of religious education on the basis of the 'reasonableness' of religious beliefs, and therefore for the promotion of a way of life ('personal formation') consonant with those beliefs, thereby rejecting the frequently made opposition to such on the basis of its being 'indoctrinatory'.

1
TEACHING RELIGIOUS EDUCATION
Changing conceptions of RE

The book begins with the changing conceptions of religious education arising from an increasingly secular context and the weakening of a religious culture within society as a whole. Special reference is made to England and Wales, but philosophical issues concerning the relation between faith and reason, raised through this context, have wider significance, exemplified significantly by reference to Ireland. This has been, and remains, an important debate, understandably as societies increasingly lack a common understanding of the place of religion within them, and without examination of a rational basis for the foundations of religious belief, and thereby for religious education and formation in schools. It is particularly relevant, given the report in England and Wales of the Commission on Religious Education, but also in Ireland, given the divestment of some schools from the Catholic sector and the creation of Educate Together Schools and Community National Schools embracing a variety of religious and world views.

Introduction – growing doubts

The teaching of religious education is probably the most contentious issue in the curriculum of schools in Britain but no doubt also elsewhere.[1] This is not surprising, as we have seen the shift over several decades from the assumption that schools operate within a Christian culture, which is permeated by specific beliefs and which has created what the philosopher Charles Taylor, 2007, referred to as the 'horizons of significance' (the reference points in our moral lives), to a secular culture in which such beliefs are ignored or challenged. No longer can it be said, as Lady Olga Maitland declared in a speech in the British Parliament's House of Commons in 1962,

> the time has come to stop being apologetic about being a Christian country, we should not allow unbelievers to undermine our traditions.

However, the voices of the unbelievers (the secularists and the humanists) are increasingly influential, and sometimes hostile, affecting what are seen to be the aims of education, the place of religion on the curriculum, and the continued existence within the public sector of faith-based schools. Such a curriculum (it is assumed) should be primarily concerned with the advancement of knowledge and understanding (not with religious formation), and *No More Faith Schools* is a national campaign coordinated by the National Secular Society and dedicated to bringing about an end to state-funded Faith Schools. If religious beliefs do not have a 'knowledge base', then they should not be taught as if they do. Thus, Professor Paul Hirst argued in an influential paper, arising out of his advocacy of the different forms of knowledge as the bases of what should be taught:

> There has already emerged in our society a view of education, a concept of education, which makes the whole idea of Christian education a kind of nonsense and the search for a Christian approach to, or philosophy of, education, a huge mistake.
>
> *(Hirst, 1965)*

Religious education, therefore, as a subject on the curriculum, would seem not to have the one feature which other subjects would claim to have, namely, the basis in a form of knowledge where distinctions can be made between true and false claims as to what should be believed.

It was not ever thus. Olga Maitland's later plea to Parliament in 1993 to maintain the traditions of a Christian culture assumed the truth of the religious beliefs which permeated the social fabric and which would be re-enforced through the teaching and assemblies in all schools. Indeed, that had inevitably been the case in the past because the religious foundations (Church of England, Non-Conformist, and, later, Roman Catholic) had provided the beginnings and development of the elementary school system in England and Wales from 1833 onwards, when grants were given to existing religious school foundations by the Privy Council.

There was inevitably opposition from those who, not having religious beliefs, saw no place for the teaching of religion in schools. The Secular League, for instance, formed in 1907, insisted that the teaching of religion was not the responsibility of the State. But, much earlier, to meet such objections, the 1870 Education Act created school boards for the overall distribution of grants to schools, which were now to include 'School Board schools' with no religious affiliation. The Act furthermore incorporated the Cowper-Temple clause with regard to the new non-denominational schools, namely,

> No religious catechism or religious formulary which is distinctive of any particular denomination shall be taught in the school.

However, even in the denominational schools, which would be the only elementary schools in most areas, there was to be a 'conscience clause' whereby parents could remove children from religious assemblies and instruction.

Therefore, one can see the increasing difficulty in Britain of maintaining the 'subject' of 'religious education' as a set of beliefs to be taught to all young people as a basis of a particular form of life. It would necessarily, if it were to survive, mean something different (with different challenges, as will be shown in the penultimate chapter of this book) in those schools, which were religiously affiliated, from those schools which were not. Moreover, it would inevitably mean something different in schools under different religious bodies – Church of England, Roman Catholic and Non-conformist, amongst which there were theological differences. And again it would mean something different where the 'common school' catered to pupils of very different faiths or none, in particular to the significant numbers of Muslim pupils in ethnically mixed schools.

Where there are differences, even between religious denominations, as well as between major religions (especially Christian, Muslim and Jewish), concerning the content of, and knowledge base for, religious education, doubts begin to arise about it being a *form of knowledge* and thereby a legitimate candidate for a curriculum subject – even though, on the other hand, the subject of 'history' and the explanations and facts which it offers are often a matter of dispute amongst historians and philosophers of history. But such epistemological disputes fail to dislodge history from the 'forms of knowledge' which have become the basis of the 'academic curriculum'.

On the other hand, despite theological differences (and prior to Britain becoming a significantly multi-ethnic society), Archbishop Temple wrote in 1942,

> We ought as Christians to be concerned about the whole of the education process. I am quite sure that the raising of the school-leaving age will of itself do more to make permanent the religious influence of the schools than anything that can be done with directly denominational purpose.

Such 'religious influence' would require 'religious education' to be part of the curriculum as well as part of the character formation through daily assemblies.

Changing conceptions of religious education

It is important for the purposes of this book to see how the very conception of religious education thus began to change (from 'directly denominational purpose' to 'religious influence') once the foundations of Christian belief gradually came to be widely doubted within a more secular society, and even interpreted differently between the different religious communities. Seeds of that change are reflected in the words of the Spens Report which preceded the 1944 Education Act. Emphasis was certainly given to the importance of knowing the Scripture, which presumably would be seen as common to the different denominations but also a considerable cultural heritage even for the unbelievers (Mr. Gove, for instance, when Secretary of State, ensured that a copy of the King James' Bible was despatched to every school for that declared reason). But, as Spens Report, 1938, Chapter 5 affirmed,

> We believe that there is a wide and genuine recognition of the value and importance of religious instruction and teaching of Scripture in schools, and

that the time is favourable for a fresh consideration of the place that they should occupy in the education of boys and girls of secondary school age.

But, as Gearon (2013, p. 109) commented,

> Given the subsequent history of the scriptural-theological approaches, and the place of the Bible in religious education, such optimism seems somewhat misplaced.

Nonetheless, whether or not such scriptural studies should form a basis for religious education, the Spens Report of 1938 felt confident to conclude that

> no boy or girl can be counted as properly educated unless he or she has been made aware of the fact of the existence of a religious interpretation of life.

Being 'made aware of the fact' is one step away from the teaching of religious beliefs or of a religious way of life into which the learners are to be initiated. It would seem to be no more than recognising that an appreciation of such an 'interpretation of life' is important – one aspect, one might say, of 'general education'.

Differences thereby appeared between those who saw religious education to be an initiation into a form of knowledge (including scriptural knowledge) as a basis for living and personal formation, and those who, doubtful of there being a foundation for such a form of knowledge, argued increasingly that religious education needed ulterior purposes other than the nurturing of religious beliefs. The 1944 Education Act (which applied to England and Wales, not to Scotland and Northern Ireland which had their own devolved powers over education) distinguished between County or Community schools (with no religious affiliation) and Voluntary schools ('controlled' or 'aided'). This gave rise to the continuing debate about the nature of the subject within the system of education. Certainly, a daily assembly of a religious nature was legally required of all schools, as also was 'an agreed syllabus' for the teaching of religion, but to be locally agreed – except in the case of the Voluntary Aided schools which would have their own distinctive syllabuses based on the specific religious beliefs of the Catholic Church.

The slow evolution thereafter of the national conception of religious education was reflected in the 1988 Education Act, which, although stipulating it as a 'basic subject', nonetheless, unlike in all other subjects of the new 'national curriculum', gave no national guidelines regarding content, progression or assessment. Religion was no longer equated with Christianity. Therefore, local SACREs (Standing Advisory Councils on Religious Education) were required to reflect the diverse religious and indeed non-religious interests of the area in promoting the particular content, materials and suggestions for teaching. Those diverse religious interests would now include the increasing number of pupils who came from very different religious traditions.

It is not surprising, therefore, that this gradual reshaping of religious education as a subject on the school curriculum should result in its no longer being taught in many schools. According to the Report of the National Association of Teachers of Religion, more than a quarter of England's secondary schools do not offer religious education (reported on BBC, 17th September 2017).

The problem is that, where there would seem to be no solid foundation for the specific beliefs underpinning religious education, it cannot be taught as if there were. Indeed, the difficulty is enlarged where such a large proportion of young people show no interest in participating in religious practice and worship. Thus, in the recent British Social Attitudes Survey (BSA, 2018), less than 2% of 18–24 year olds now identify with the Church of England, which, being the national church, has had so much influence on the maintenance of religious education through the several Education Acts. This reflects a steady decrease not only in the practice of religion but also in its perceived significance in the trend towards a secular society. Certainly, it would thereby seem educationally unjustifiable to use schools to nurture particular beliefs as if they had a widely accepted firm foundation. Such a 'confessional' approach would appear to be opposite from an educational one. It would be seen as 'intellectual and cultic indoctrination, equating it with "dogmatic"', according to Schools Council, 1971, Working Paper 36, *Religious Education in Secondary Schools*.

Therefore, understandably, Andrew Wright (2010, p. 131) poses the question:

> What might local faith communities reasonably expect of religious education in the state schools of a secular democracy?

Rescue attempts – changing the nature of religious education

The key issue, therefore, concerns the nature of religious *beliefs* – the grounds on which they can be justified in terms of evidence for their claimed truth. The secular opposition to religious education, as it has been traditionally maintained, was that such beliefs (such 'phenomena') are not supported by reason, and therefore to teach them, or to teach ways of living as if they were supported by good reasons, would be to indoctrinate. The same issues were inevitably raised in the United States where the First Amendment of the Constitution, as was declared in 1791, guaranteed religious freedom through the separation of the state from religion. Hence, according to Miller et al. (2013, p. 4),

> The current thinking in the U.S. tends to emphasise a sharp distinction between learning about religion and religious indoctrination.

Furthermore, as is indicated in the penultimate section of this chapter, similar issues are beginning to emerge in Ireland resulting from the increasing secularisation of that society.

One result of this growing critique of the religious formation being promoted through formal education is the accusation which speaks of the example of repetitive indoctrination,

> foisting upon the individual a point of view without giving him as full a picture of the salient facts as possible and the freedom to come to his own conclusions.
>
> *(Hilliard, 1963; see Copley, 2008, p. 67)*

Therefore, resulting from such opposition within an increasingly secular society, we have seen different and interesting ways in which support for some form of religious education (the recognition of this 'phenomenon') might be maintained in the schools' curricula, even though not officially formulated or even enthusiastically undertaken in all schools. These different ways are more extensively summarised by Gearon (2013, pp. 104–134) in his book, *Master Class in Religious Education*, in which he refers to 'the paradigm shift', reflected in the writings of several religious educators. The following points very briefly summarise some such attempts.

(i) Maintenance of values inherited from the Christian tradition

A series of reports from within the Church of England (Durham Report, 1970, *The Fourth R*; Dearing Report, 2001, *Way Ahead: Church of England schools in the new millennium*; Chadwick Report, 2012, *Going for Growth: transformation for children, young persons and the Church*) argued for the importance of maintaining the national educational system, the values derived from the Christian inheritance and transmitted through the generations, especially in view of the increasing domination

> by a secularist viewpoint indicative of an increasing utilitarian and materialist approach to education in which market economics would become the overriding ethos of schools.
>
> *(Chadwick, 1997)*

Certainly it would seem and could be argued that permeating any society is a 'family of values', which can so easily be diminished by other social forces unless they are carefully nurtured and enforced. Thus, a religious form of life (often only implicit for many but reflected in customary practices) provided the continuing stimulus (the 'horizons of significance', as related by Charles Taylor, 2007, for those social values.

On the other hand, once the grounds or foundations for those traditional values either are denied or no longer hold the interest of the population (back to the statistics given in the latest British Social Attitudes survey, referred to above), then it may seem inappropriate to see them located in religious education.

(ii) Social cohesion: understanding other people and cultures

The Swan Report in 1985, *Education for All*, (concerned with 'the education of children from ethnic minority groups') argued that the value of religious education lay in its potential for developing multi-cultural cohesion rather than having value in its own right. Such an aim became increasingly common in various influential documents. In 2009, a Faith and Education Seminar at the Commonwealth Headquarters in London argued for the heightened place of religious education

> to promote tolerance, respect, enlightened moderation and friendship amongst people of different faiths and cultures, as well as explore initiatives to promote mutual understanding and respect in the commonwealth.
>
> *(Gearon, 2013, p. 24)*

This, as Gearon earlier explains (p. 18), is in keeping with similarly motivated statements from international agencies, for example, what were referred to as the *Toledo Guiding Principles*, pointing to the

> importance for young people to acquire a better understanding of the role that religions play in today's pluralistic world.

Such importance is increased in the multi-ethnic society which has now developed, especially the new Muslim diaspora, where, according to the Pew Research Center, 2001 (quoted by Wilkinson, 2015), nearly half of the 2.7 million Muslims in Britain are under the age of 25, which means that by 2000 there are likely to be 5.5 million Muslim British. Understanding sympathetically the facts here of such a large number would seem to be necessary for social cohesion, as indeed endorsed by Ofsted, 2007, in the significantly entitled report, *Making Sense of Religion*:

> RE cannot ignore its role in fostering community cohesion built on shared values and shared public cultures.
>
> *(p. 40)*

But such a worthwhile objective and justification for the development and practice of 'religious education' does not entail the teaching of religion as a form of knowledge or as a set of commitments for how life should be lived based upon firm foundations. Rather does it have a more political purpose in promoting cultural understanding and social cohesion within more multi-cultural civic societies.

On the other hand, it remains unclear how a 'Cook's tour' of different religious faiths (each one of which, as in the case of Christianity and Islam, is to be divided into different, and sometimes antagonistic, 'denominations') can, in the absence of examination of the truth claims of the different faiths or of a distinctive spiritual dimension (as reflected in ritual), provide much insight for cultural understanding.

(iii) Phenomenological or interpretive understanding

Therefore, emphasis shifted in some cases from the teaching of religion as one amongst several 'forms of knowledge' to the teaching of it as a 'phenomenon', which is seen to be of cultural interest and significance. Thus, Jean Holm, 1975, in *Teaching Religion in School*, argued that the

> common denominator of all religions was that religion has always been an important *phenomenon* (this author's italics) of human experience, expressed as a need to make sense of the world, to affirm that there is a purpose not of human making, that the structure of reality is something that human beings belong to rather than something that belongs to them.
>
> *(quoted in Copley, 2008, p. 110)*

To understand such cultures, different from one's own, would require insight into the distinctive religious practices and beliefs. This in turn would require some suspension of judgment concerning the truth or falsity of specific beliefs, including one's own – or 'bracketing them off' – as the focus would be upon the religious consciousness which is illustrated vividly in the arts, music and literature, which is embedded within the different religious beliefs and practices, and which is something to be understood in its own terms. Thus, for example, as argued by Brown, 2001, in his book, significantly entitled, *The Death of Christian Britain*,

> Only when we can 'bracket out' ourselves, our preconceived notions and our particular values, and concentrate on what, for example, a Muslim feels when he prays to Allah . . . will we begin to appreciate and understand the essence of Islam.

The concept of 'bracketing off' is central to the philosophical account of phenomenology as developed by Husserl, to be explained further in Chapter 3.

Such insights, if they were to be had, would provide the opportunity and possibly the stimulus for the pupils to explore further – to make links between religious accounts, on the one hand, and their own experiences and lives on the other. In so doing they might seek (and be encouraged to do so) to explore the grounds for maintaining such beliefs and living according to them. They could become 'insiders', 'interpreting', and thereby developing, the understanding gained within their own consciousness of the issues addressed. Therefore, there was emphasis given to pupils' own inner experience, too often neglected in a curriculum in thrall to the 'transmission of knowledge'. As Jack Priestley (1992) argued,

> The great purpose of education should be to give people greater reliance on the validity of their own inward and private experience.

And so, as he explained in an earlier work (1985, p. 116), in a paper significantly entitled, 'Towards finding the hidden curriculum: a consideration of the spiritual dimension of experience in curriculum planning', learning to use religious language

> may well involve an intellectual awareness of the world outside but it does so for the purpose of evoking the world inside us.

That 'own inward and private experience' would be enhanced by exposure to others' accounts through poetry, art and narratives, as illustrated in Chapter 2, following. Thus, religious education might be expected to help pupils reflect critically on the truth of religious beliefs (Christian, Jewish, Islamic and other beliefs) and how their claimed truth is relevant today. Such an interpretive approach in helping learners to find their own way may not necessarily be undertaken in separation from the religious life – namely, the context of ritual and prayer which would in the past have provided the experiential background to critical reflection.

The epistemological significance of such an 'interpretive approach' will be examined in Chapter 3 of this book. But it is important to see how, especially developed by Professor Ninian Smart (1968) in his book, *Secular Education and the Logic of Religion*, such a non-dogmatic approach to religious education might reconcile, on the one hand, the 'confessional' approach of teaching which once prevailed, and, on the other hand, the religiously trivial account of different religions (and non-religious world views) seemingly required in a secular society. As Smart argued,

> Religious education must transcend the informative . . . in the direction of initiation into understanding the meaning of, and questions about, the truth and worth of, religion.

Such 'interpretive accounts of experience' (the phenomenological approach) became consolidated by the Qualifications and Curriculum Authority, 2004, *Non-statutory Guidance for Religious Education*, and again in 2010. In so doing, pupils would reflect on different views of truth represented within and across religious traditions as well as consider the function of religious activity in pupils' lives (see, for example, Jackson, 1997, p. 126).

It has been argued by Wilkinson (2015, p. 209), in what he refers to as the 'interfaith mode', that ontological realism (by which is meant the existence of God as the source of spiritual experience)

> is the mode at which the nature of spiritual and religious phenomena is examined ontologically in the classroom without reference to a religious tradition. It is the mode of looking at the field of absolute concerns for life of the spirit generated by the universal quest for the meaning of life.

It is this form of entry into religious understanding and therefore education, as developed at length in the following chapter, which is identified as one of the 'challenges for religious education' in the penultimate chapter of this book.

12 Teaching religious education

Nonetheless, it is important to reflect further (as in Chapter 3) on the philosophical basis for such an understanding of religion and thus of religious education. Here, and especially in the influential work of Smart, 1968, there was an attempt to find a middle ground between the more 'confessional' approach, which once prevailed, but which no longer seemed acceptable in a liberal and secular society, and the purely secular approach which discounted such a truth-based religious form of life.

(iv) Spiritual insight

Both the 1944 and the 1988 Education Acts required all schools to develop the spiritual well-being of all pupils, even though the nature of religious education was increasingly being questioned. Hence, there was an increasing struggle to preserve, and hence define, 'spirituality' within general education without its foundation depending on religious understanding and form of life. Thus, the National Curriculum Council in 1993 (p. 2) explained that spirituality

> has to do with relationships with other people and, for believers, with God. It has to do with the universal search for individual identity – with our response to the challenging experiences such as death, suffering, beauty and encounters with good and evil. It is to do with the search for meaning and purpose in life and for the values by which to live.

Here, therefore, we have an argument for a place in school life where there might be 'the search for meaning and purpose in life', something which traditionally would have been provided by a religious tradition and teaching but which now has to be undertaken in the absence of such tradition – although such a search might lead to the rediscovery of the religious dimension to life and personal fulfilment. The importance attached to this for the schools' curricula was reflected in the inspectorate's proposal to inspect 'spiritual development' in all schools (Ofsted, 1994).

However, as Carr (1996) pointed out,

> the recommendation to 'develop spiritual insight', especially in the absence of a religious context, is fraught with 'rival conceptions of spiritual education'.

First, 'developing spiritual insight', according to Carr, would seem to refer in these government and HMI documents to a subjective experience which one might have in relation to a particular scene or event, and with regard to which one might speak of the 'sublime' or the 'ineffable'. Thereby the 'spiritual' easily becomes equated with what may be referred to as an aesthetic experience or appreciation. But in the arts, such as painting and music, there is a tradition of criticism into which the students can be initiated in order to develop their aesthetic sensibility; it would seem to be not entirely a subjective matter. From paying attention to such a tradition (listening, say, to Bach's Mass in B Minor) one might gain a spiritual experience, but that endows a meaning beyond the purely aesthetic experience. The music would mean something different to the person to whom the Mass embodied a religious belief and attitude.

Second, therefore, 'spiritual', as different from 'aesthetic' or the 'sublime', traditionally implies a distinctive kind of understanding of experience, and such an understanding is grasped within a tradition developed, not only on the basis of religious texts but also of their being lived by particular people. There are 'spiritual readings' of those who have come to be recognised as saints ('holy people') within religious traditions. It may seem difficult to understand what 'spiritual' *distinctively* means, so it is argued, outside such traditions of religious teaching and living, and the recognition of a reality which 'transcends' the here and now of the material world

Therefore, Carr further argues:

> The only way to make much sense of spiritual education on a significant part of the school curriculum is via the engagement of young people with some serious tradition of spiritual reflection or enquiry through which they might come to appreciate the nature of genuine spiritual concerns and questions – as well as something of what acknowledged past masters of a tradition may have accomplished in trying to address such concerns.

The issues are well summarised by Wright (1998, p. 24) through distinguishing between, on the one hand, the 'anthropological definition of spiritual education', as legislated in the 1988 Education Act, (namely, a common universal definition into which all pupils might be inducted whatever their religious traditions or none) and, on the other hand, the theological definition 'with its tighter focus on human knowledge and experience related to God', and hence, as with Carr above, 'the engagement of young people with some serious tradition of spiritual reflection or enquiry'.

These issues will be dealt with in much greater length in Chapter 6 of this book, in particular how 'the spiritual' makes sense in what Gill and Thomson, 2014, refer to as the 'thinner meaning' of the word, but is related to its 'thicker meaning' within a religious tradition and form of life. As will be indicated in the following chapter, what might be referred to, at least initially, as a 'subjective state of mind' (the 'thinner meaning', and thereby easily dismissed) might indicate and lead on to the postulation of a presence which transcends the phenomenal world and which comes to be embodied in ritual and a form of life (the 'thicker meaning').

But, of course, the second sense raises important questions about the relation of belief to relevant reasons for such beliefs in a way that the first sense does not. Hence, it is necessary to return to this in Chapter 9 as one of the 'challenges for religious education' in schools, especially Faith Schools.

A final or interim conclusion to the problem?

To help draw conclusions from these and other attempts to redefine religious education and to recommend a way forward, the Religious Education Council for

England and Wales established in 2016 a Commission on Religious Education (CRE) to provide a thorough review of the subject. The Commission reported finally in September 2017. Its remit was to review the legal, education and policy framework for religious education to be studied up to age 16, thereby both to inform policy makers and 'to prepare pupils for modern life in Britain'.

First, and significantly, it recommended that the subject should be renamed as 'Religion and World Views', the content of which

> must reflect the complex, diverse and plural nature of world-views drawing from a range of religious, philosophical, spiritual, and other approaches to life, including different traditions within Christianity, Buddhism, Hinduism, Islam, Judaism, and Sikhism, non-religious world-views and concepts including humanism, secularism, atheism and agnosticism.
>
> *(CRE, 2017)*

Therefore, with the humanists being represented on the Commission and with humanism being one of the world views alongside Christianity and other religions in the proposed curriculum, Andrew Copson (President of Humanism UK), 2018, was reported as referring to

> a once-in-a-generation opportunity to save the academically serious teaching of religious and non-religious world-views in our schools.

Such a radical, though no doubt temporary, conclusion to the long-maturing nature and role of 'religious education' inevitably had its critics. The Vice-President of the Board of Deputies of British Jews declared that the report was 'fundamentally flawed'. It was underpinned by the

> dilution of religious education through the inclusion of world-views in an already tight timetable. . . . This might be seen as an attempt by those hostile to faith to push their agenda of undermining the rigour in religious education at a time when faith literacy could not be more important.

The Catholic Education Council similarly commented,

> not so much an attempt to improve religious education as to fundamentally change its character. . . . The quality of religious education is not improved by teaching less religion.

In particular, it would seem to lack the sort of clarity which would be essential if, as the Ofsted Discussion Paper (referred to above) or the National Curriculum Council recommendations of 1997 argued, the 'spiritual dimension' were to have a place on the curriculum and to be inspected, especially in the light of what has been stated above by Wright and Priestley, to which we shall need to return in Chapter 9.

Ireland: the changing landscape

Until recently 95% of Irish primary schools were Faith Schools, 90% of these being under the trusteeship of the local Catholic Diocese or the Religious Orders. Of the nation's post-primary schools, just over 50% were not under that trusteeship. But today Ireland has become a more secular society – a rising number of young people around Dublin identify themselves as non-religious, Mass attendances on Sundays have declined considerably and membership of the religious orders which were responsible for many schools has declined. Furthermore, Irish society has been affected by the immigration of many people of different religions or none.

Therefore, there have been two sorts of challenges to the influence of the religious dominance over education.

The first challenge lies in the call to divest the control of some schools (especially much-needed new ones) from the Catholic diocese, especially in the Dublin area, so that there can be greater parental choice. Indeed, it is sought to repeal the Act which allows schools to operate the 'Catholics First Policy' (see *The Tablet* 30.10.15). Hence, there is the development of EDT (Educate Together) schools, with an 'ethical education curriculum' rather than a religiously based one, and also Community National Schools under the patronage of local Education and Training Boards claiming to provide an inclusive education for all children, irrespective of religious belief, although enabling the students to separate into their respective religious groups for their distinctive faith formation.

The second challenge lies in the nature of the religious education even within the great majority of schools attached to the diocese and their parishes. In his address on *The Church of the Future* (March 2019, reported in The Tablet 30.3.19), Archbishop Martin of Dublin said,

> There are fundamental fault lines within the current structure for Catholic schools that are not being addressed, and unattended fault-lines inevitably generate destructive energies. Irish culture has drifted from being an enlarged faith community into a heavily secularised culture. For many, faith no longer plays a major role in their lives and they feel that this in no way compromises their ability to be good, honest and caring people. [Catholic education], despite the investment in the structures of school-based religious education and enormous goodwill, was not producing the results that it set out to achieve.

Thus, according to Sean O'Connell in *The Furrow*, there is a failure of Church leadership 'to confront the challenges of faith formation in what is now a post-Christian society'.

The crucial issue – the role of reason and truth in faith formation

What we have seen, in this account, is an evolving understanding of 'religious education' in the curriculum of schools as the consequence not only of the gradual decline in society of the religious beliefs and practices upon which such teaching would be based, but also of the increasingly secular nature of society which has replaced the dominant religious culture. That secularisation assumes that such religious beliefs lack ultimate justification, and, within a liberal tradition of education, should not promote beliefs as true, the meaning and truth of which are widely challenged. The *truth* of such beliefs cannot be shown, so it is argued. Religious faiths do not have a firm rational foundation. Hence, to teach them as if they have a rational foundation would be to indoctrinate. As one RE commentator observed, most RE teachers dodge the 'is it true?' question with a response like, 'Many people believe it is true'.

At most, the curriculum must be confined to *teaching about* the different beliefs as part of understanding the broader cultures which affect society – although, in so doing, opening up the possibility (to the more curious) of yet further exploration and significance of such beliefs. Therefore, the words of the Bristol Agreed Syllabus of 1960, included in a section entitled, 'Is the Bible true?', seem somewhat odd 60 years later.

> The ultimate question that must be raised is this: is Christianity wholly true and the other religions wholly false, or can we say that while there is truth in all the great religions, Christianity supplants what is false and completes what is true in all the others.

At the centre, therefore, of the curriculum issues concerning the nature, and indeed the very existence, of religious education is the philosophical question concerning their truth and rationality. Can the bases of religious belief and practice be shown to be true, and thereby the teaching of them both assume and demonstrate such truth? If not, then it would seem that religious education at the most must be concerned not with the truth of its basic propositions, but (as argued by the Swan Report, 1968) with their significance in our understanding of different societies or cultural groups within society. They are but part of the cultural background with which an educated person should be familiar.

It is this issue with which the following chapters are concerned. Are distinctively religious thought and practice reasonable, that is, having foundations which can be shown to be based on good reasons? It is a question which, with rare exceptions, seems to have been dodged in the different attempts to rescue religious education and certainly in the latest report of the Commission on Religious Education. But, as Jackson (1997, p. 126) declared,

> Young people have the right to study and reflect on different views of truth represented within and across religious traditions as well as considering the function of religious activity in persons' lives.

Therefore, as Wright, 2007 (pp. 90–97), seemingly a little suspicious of the force or value of the interpretive or phenomenological approach and concerned by the 'eclipse of truth', asks how one might cope with the different religious understandings and yet maintain the notion of truth, because,

> convinced that religious truth claims are not open to rational evaluation, or fearful of exhibiting any hint of indoctrination, many religious educators have embraced strategic designs to avoid confronting the possibility that one or other religions or secular world-views might actually be true. The cumulative effect of these strategies has been to draw the cognitive sting from religious belief and thus reduce learning about religion to a neutral process incapable of having any direct impact on the lives of pupils.
>
> *(p. 93)*

Thus, it gradually lost its identity as an introduction to a 'form of knowledge' about God, Christ and the Bible (that is, to a way of thinking based on well-rehearsed rational grounds from which one might look differently at the prevailing 'horizons of significance').

This was put more dramatically at the political level by Lady Olga Maitland, M.P. for Sutton and Cheam, who campaigned for a return to a thorough understanding of Christianity, to its beliefs and to its way of life – referring in the *Church of England Newspaper* (12.3.94) to the current practice of religious education as an 'Ultimate Betrayal' and 'RE all at sea', and asserting in a speech to the House of Commons,

> Far too many syllabuses are not complying with . . . [the requirement to teach Christianity], which is why, according to a MORI poll, 44% of school leavers leave school without a proper understanding of what happened even on Easter Day.
>
> *(Hansard, 3.3.93)*

That was in 1993. Since then, religious education has drifted further away from an understanding not only of Christianity but also, in many cases, of the meaning and significance of religion. As Wintergill stated in 1995,

> There has been a tendency to apologise for RE or to camouflage it as multicultural education, environmental education, or some generalised path to self-understanding. Worst still many primary teachers, encouraged to teach RE for the first time, have been told that 'RE is everything' with *Dogger* and *The Velvetine* [sic] *Rabbit* acquiring almost the status of sacred texts for key stage 1.

Thus, he continues,

> religious education should deal with truth with a capital 'T' – not found in individual experience but in public linguistic traditions and communities that uphold these truth claims and make them alive for their adherents.

However, to what extent does this fit with the phenomenological approach to religious education which tended to seek an 'essentialist' understanding of the different religions – that is, the common element of which specific religions are but the manifestations?

Crucial, therefore, to our examination of religious education, its nature and its acceptability within a liberal and increasingly secular society, are, first, the nature of religious faith, its truth and its reasonableness, and, second, the common factor between different religious traditions, faiths and experiences – their shared reasonableness, and a major 'challenge for religious education', to be taken up in Chapter 9. But, to meet that challenge, it is necessary in the following three chapters to consider the philosophical issues concerned with religious knowledge and understanding – whether or not there is a disconnect between faith and reason.

Note

1 The references are to education acts and official papers for England and Wales, not for Scotland and Northern Ireland, which, under devolved control for education, created their different systems, although the issues raised here about the nature of religious education remain relevant.

Bibliography

Brown, C., 2001, *The Death of Christian Britain*, London: Routledge.
BSA, 2018, *British Social Attitudes Survey*, London: The King's Fund.
Carr, D., 1995, 'Towards a distinctive conception of spiritual education', *Oxford Review of Education*, 21 (1).
Carr, D., 1996, 'Rival conceptions of spiritual education', *Journal of Philosophy of Education*, 30 (2).
Chadwick, P., 1997, *Shifting Alliances: Church and State in English Education*, London: Cassell.
Chadwick Report, 2012, *Going for Growth: Transformation for Children, Young Persons and the Church*, London: SPCK.
Cooling, T., 2010, *Doing God in Education*, London: Theos Think Tank.
Copley, T., 2008, *Teaching Religion: Sixty Years of Teaching Religion in England and Wales*, new edition, University of Exeter Press.
CRE (Commission on Religious Education), 2017, *Religious Education for All*, London: Religious Education Council for England and Wales.
Dearing Report, 2001, *Way Ahead: Church of England Schools in the New Millennium*, London: Church House Publications.
Durham Report, 1970, *The Fourth R; Report of the Commission on RE in Schools*, London: SPCK.
Gearon, L., 2013, *MasterClass in Religious Education: Transforming Teaching and Learning*, London: Bloomsbury.
Gill, S., and Thomson, G., eds., 2014, *Redefining Religious Education: Spirituality for Human Flourishing*, New York: Palgrave Macmillan.
Grimmitt, M., ed., 2000, *Pedagogies of Religious Education: Case Studies in in the Research and Development of Good Pedagogic Practice in RE*, Great Wakering: McCrimmon.
Grimmitt, M., 2010, *Religious Education and Social Community Cohesion*, Great Wakering: McCrimmon.
Hilliard, E.W., 1963, *The Teacher and Religion*, Cambridge: James Clarke.

Hirst, P.H., 1965, 'Morals, religion and the maintained school', in *British Journal of Educational Studies*, 14.
Holm, J., 1975, *Teaching Religion in School*, Oxford: Oxford University Press.
Jackson, R., 1997, *Religious Education: An Interpretive Approach*, London: Hodder and Stoughton.
Miller, J., O'Grady, K., and McKenna, U., 2013, *Religion in Education: Innovation in International Research*, London: Routledge.
NCC (National Curriculum Council), 1993, *Spiritual and Moral Development*, London: Routledge.
Ofsted, 1994, *Spiritual, Moral, Social and Cultural Development*, Discussion Paper.
Ofsted, 2007, *Making Sense of Religion: A Report on Religious Education in Schools and the Impact of Locally Agreed Syllabuses*, London: Office for Standards in Education.
Priestley, J., 1985, 'Towards finding the hidden curriculum: A consideration of the spiritual dimension of experience in curriculum planning', *British Journal of Religious Education*, 7 (3).
Priestley, J., 1992, 'Whitehead revisited – religion and education: an organic whole', in Watson, B., ed., *Priorities in Religious Education: A Model for the 1990s and Beyond*, London: Falmer Press.
Qualifications and Curriculum Authority, 2004, *Non-statutory Guidance for Religious Education*, London: QCA.
Qualifications and Curriculum Authority, 2010, *Religious Education in English Schools: New Statutory Guidance*, London: Virgo.
REDCo Project (Religious Education Council for England and Wales), *Religion in Education: A Contribution to Dialogue or a Factor of Conflict*, European Commission.
Schools Council, 1971, *Religious Education in Secondary Schools*, Schools Council Working Paper 36.
Smart, N., 1968, *Secular Education and the Logic of Religion*, London: Faber and Faber.
Spens Report, 1938, *Report of the Consultative Committee on Secondary Education*, London: Board of Education.
Swan Report, 1985, *Education for All*, London: HMSO.
Taylor, C., 2007, *A Secular Age*, Harvard University Press.
Wilkinson, M., 2015, *A Fresh Look at Islam in a Multi-Faith World*, London: Routledge.
Wintersgill, E., 1995, 'The case of the missing models: Exploding the myths', in *Resource*, 18 (1).
Wright, A., 1998, *Spiritual Pedagogy*, Culham College Institute.
Wright, A., 2000, *Spirituality and Education*, Routledge.
Wright, A., 2007, *Critical Religious Education, Multiculturalism and the Pursuit of Truth*, Cardiff University Press, pp. 196–200.
Wright, A., 2010, 'Community, diversity and truth', in Grimmitt, M., ed., *Religious Education and Social Community Cohesion*, Great Wakering, UK: McCrimmons.

2
FAITH
Meaning and reasonableness

It is important at the start of such a philosophical examination to identify what is meant by having 'a faith', namely: (i) the beliefs which constitute that faith and (ii) the way of life and commitments which such beliefs entail. At this early stage of the argument, it may help to point to what Rudolf Otto referred to in 'The Idea of the Holy', or to what William James revealed in 'The Varieties of Religious Experience', or to Emile Pascal's 'mysterium tremendum' in his 'Les Pensees', or to Mohammad's response to the revelations on Mount Hira, or to the way of life presented in the 'Torah' – namely, that deep-seated sense of the 'numinous' which arises in so many cultures. However, criticisms have to be faced in the light of challenges to the truth of such beliefs, especially within the context of education, and therefore to the reasonableness of such beliefs and of consequent commitments. This is where the epistemological issues of having, and therefore teaching, a faith are raised, prior to further analysis (in Chapters 3 and 4). Can a belief be seen to be reasonable when based upon a powerful sense of 'the holy', even where it seems that it cannot be proved to be true?

What is 'faith'?

A seemingly obvious answer to this question would be that 'faith' signifies a belief or a set of beliefs which someone holds. But the Oxford English Dictionary refers not to just any kind of beliefs, but those 'founded on authority' – in particular 'beliefs in religious doctrines' and 'spiritual apprehension of divine truth *apart from proof*' (this author's italics). Indeed, having a particular faith is often *contrasted* with beliefs which are based on reason, reflected in Kierkgaard's 'leap of faith', which conveys the idea that God cannot be known objectively but only subjectively by intuition (Kierkegaard, 1844, Philosophical Fragments). Thus, where such faith provides a basis for educational practice, it comes to be seen by its critics as a matter of indoctrination.

However, such a narrow understanding of 'faith' (namely, as contrasted with beliefs based on reason) is misleading. A person may develop a set of beliefs (moral, aesthetic and philosophical as well as religious) through reflection, or through what the Spens Report, 1938, with reference to the justification of religious education in schools) spoke of as 'an *appreciation* of a religious interpretation of life', or through what the NCC Report, 1993, spoke of as a 'search for meaning and purpose in life'.

On the other hand, as John Henry Newman, 1870, asked in *Grammar of Assent*, how can religious belief be justified, given that the evidence for its conclusions seems so inadequate to the degree of commitment? His answer, as indeed that of others, is that faith may arise from many different sources, and it may grow through continuing reflection and experience, as, for example, in the growing force of a moral consciousness (as developed in Chapter 5 of this book), which cannot be derived from empirical experience (see Chapter 4). Hence, in his *University Sermons*, Newman admits and argues that

> reason may be limited in its power, but unlimited in its range. It reaches to the ends of the universe, and to the throne of God beyond them; it brings in knowledge, whether clear or uncertain, still knowledge in whatever degree of perfection, from every side; but at the same time, with the characteristic that it obtains it indirectly, not directly.

Philosophical thinking has always had a key role to play in what Newman referred to as 'knowledge in whatever degrees of perfection' and in critical reflection on, and clarification of, religious experiences of different kinds. In *The Consolations of Philosophy*, the 5th-century philosopher Boethius referred to philosophy as 'the lady handmaiden of theology' – the continuing reflection on what one believes (tentatively or otherwise, and from whatever sources), clarifying what is meant, and engaged in critical examination of those beliefs as they are, and have been, systematically developed within a tradition. St. Anselm's renowned statement ('Fides quaerens intellectum' – faith seeking understanding) pointed to the essential part philosophical thinking plays in criticising and clarifying faith claims in the light of further evidence, critical argument and reflection. Religious faiths are in many cases the product of a long tradition of such thought and criticism, into which future generations might be initiated. And in that respect they are no different from secular or humanist beliefs which increasingly provide the background to an understanding of the world and of how one might (or ought to) behave within it.

Moreover, 'having a faith' is normally understood as having a *range* of connected beliefs which are reflected in specific practices. For example, for the Christian, such beliefs would include not only belief in God and the divinity of Jesus Christ, but also the sacramental nature of the religious life, rituals of worship, and moral codes of conduct. For Muslims it would include the authority of the Qur'an and the Five Pillars of Islamic faith, namely, testifying that there is no God but Allah, and Muhammad as His messenger; praying according to a prescribed form, five times a day; fasting from dawn to sunset a whole month every lunar year; giving alms to the poor; visiting Mecca at least once in the lifetime if circumstances permit. For Jews, it would include the five books of the Torah and the stories as told through the Old Testament. Thus, having these beliefs would be embedded in ways of life with their distinctive rituals and devotional practices. This is eloquently put by Rabi Jonathan Sacks, with regard to the Jewish faith, in *The Politics of Hope*.

> This is a morality received not made. It is embedded in and reinforced by a total way of life, articulated in texts, transmitted across the generations, enacted in rituals, exemplified by members of the community, and underwritten by revelation and tradition.
>
> *(Sacks, 1997, p. 89)*

Certainly there is a 'feeling aspect' of such believing. Perhaps the accusation of irrationality, and thereby of indoctrination, lies in a predominance of such a state of mind where feelings seemingly precede and then shape the reasoning. Therefore, it is often presumed that religious faith is based on feelings rather than on acceptable or valid reasons, which clearly would raise concerns about indoctrinatory practices. This we must return to in the section below, namely, 'The rational and the non-rational', especially in terms of the feelings provoked. But it is first necessary to examine the place reason does and might legitimately play in the development of religious faith and in particular its interaction with the feeling dimension of that faith.

The idea of a 'Transcendent Being'

Philosophical questions and enquiries so often arise from a certain puzzlement over 'What do you mean by . . .?'. Too often we enter into an argument about the truth, say, of a statement before the meaning is clarified. We argue at cross-purposes. Never is that more so than in the case of statements about religious belief. Therefore, prior to considerations of the truth or otherwise of statements of religious belief, one needs to clarify the meaning of their assertion.

Let us say, therefore, that central to religious belief is the existence and the actions of a God. But it is rarely clear what is being asserted when one expresses a belief in God's existence, and surely clarity here would seem to be essential to consideration of the truth of statements about God, and indeed the 'total way of life' of which Rabbi Jonathan Sacks speaks (as quoted above).

This is not made easy if, as the medieval and still-influential philosopher Thomas Aquinas argued, knowledge of God consists in knowing *that* He is but not in knowing *what* He is. How can sense be made of such a paradox?

Let us begin with the almost universal belief (historically and culturally) that there is a Being (or Beings), which is not part of the material world that we experience through the senses, but which somehow *transcends* that world and in different ways influences it (through the act of creation, say, or through the setting of moral goals for which one should strive) – as with the ancient Greeks and the Romans, and countless other cultures, who had their gods which they honoured and whose assistance they sought in times of stress. Thus William James, in *Varieties of Religious Experience*, argues:

> As regards the origin of the Greek gods, we need not at present seek an opinion. But the whole array of our instances leads to a conclusion something like this: it is as if there were in the human consciousness a sense of reality, a feeling of objective presence, a perception of what we may call 'something there', more deep and more general than any of the special and particular senses by which the current psychology supposes existent reality to be originally revealed.

James, therefore, speaks of the 'numinous' as a primary datum of consciousness. Even Dawkins (2006), author of *The God Delusion*, agreed that there were grounds for saying that religious impulses to pray and worship are deeply rooted in the life of our species.

Of course, the universality and formative influence of belief arising from such feelings over time and across cultures are no *proof*, and inevitably suffer from the onslaught of the rationalists, especially from the 17th century onwards. The so-called arguments for there being a God seemingly do not meet the logical requirements of empirical evidence and rational procedure. I shall return in greater detail to the nature of truth, knowledge and certainty in Chapter 3, but here I wish solely to draw attention to a *phenomenon* (a 'consciousness' provoked by the referred-to feelings) which for many seems to provide the beginning of a journey towards a belief in a Transcendent Being and which in turn has certain attributes to be contemplated, though subject to philosophical examination as to their coherence.

This consciousness of a Transcendent Being, experienced but not understood, remains constant through the great religious traditions. Such, for example, would be the case with the revelation to Mohammad in 610 on Mount Hira, aware of an overwhelming and ubiquitous presence,

> And thus it is [with most people]: If thou ask them, 'Who is it that has created the heavens and the earth and made the sun and the moon subservient [to his laws] – they will surely answer al-Lah.
> *(Qur'an, 29:61)*

And this might be seen within the tradition of Islam as

> knowledge of absolute certainty, which is grasped as a whole in an intuitive sense and not through the use of reasoned argument.
> *(Hewer, 2006, p. 158, referring to the Qur'an, Q. 94.1)*

Such also would be the case of revelation of Isaiah to the Jews, speaking of the 'kaddosh' – that vision of holiness which we hear and hear again, but do not understand; see and see again but do not perceive (Isaiah 6: 10).

Again, Sikhism believes in the Being *beyond time*, and in that sense not known, but *manifested* in the spiritual life of the first Guru, Nanak, and expressed in the Brihadaranyaka Upanishad:

> From the unreal lead me to the real, from darkness lead me to light, from death lead me to immortality.

Such 'transcendence' (experienced but not understood) means, as the philosopher and theologian Bernard Lonergan (1957, p. 48) argued, 'going beyond' what is immediately present to raise further questions in an 'unrestricted desire for explanation'.

> The possibility of transcendent knowledge is the possibility of grasping intelligently and affirming reasonably a transcendental being. Another proof of the possibility lies in the fact that such intelligent grasp and reasonable affirmations occur.

An 'intelligent grasp' would seek coherent interpretive and phenomenological accounts of the *whole* of human experience. Such a phenomenon was articulated effectively by the 17th-century (but still-influential) scientist and philosopher, Emile Pascal, in which he speaks of 'the reasons of the heart' for becoming aware of a Being who *transcends* the experience of the senses as such and who has

> hidden himself from direct human knowledge; indeed, the very name he gives himself in Scripture is *Deus Absconditus* – the hidden God (Isaias 45:15). . . . God has appointed visible signs . . . to make himself known to those who seek him sincerely; . . . he has nonetheless veiled these signs in such a way that he will be discerned only by those who seek him with all their heart.
> *(Pascal, 1670, p. 427, quoted in Cottingham, 2009, p. 121)*

One must, of course, be careful here because of the logical gap between 'the reasons of the heart' and the conclusions reached (namely, 'the hidden God'), especially when the 'visible signs' are 'veiled'. But what Pascal refers to as 'the reasons of the heart' recurs again and again through literature – for example, in the sense of awe expressed by William Wordsworth's *Tintern Abbey*:

> a presence that disturbs me with the sense of elevated thoughts; a sense sublime of something far more deeply inter-fused whose dwelling is the light of setting suns,

or by John Ruskin, quoted in Otto (1923/1958, p. 215),

> Lastly, although there was no definite religious sentiment mingled with it, there was continual perception of Sanctity in the whole of nature, from the

slightest thing to the vastest; an instinctive awe, mixed with delight; an indefinable thrill, such as we imagine to indicate the presence of a disembodied spirit. I could feel this perfectly when I was alone; and then it would often make me shiver from head to foot with the joy and fear of it,

or by Gerard Manley Hopkins, whose poem, 'God's Grandeur', expresses, too, that permeating presence of the divine in surrounding nature, despite 'man's smudge':

The world is charged with the wonder of God
It will flame out, like shining from shook foil;

This strong influence of 'feeling' in the claimed awareness of something greater than man (in contrast with the materialist view increasingly assumed in the mechanical understanding of the universe inherited from the Enlightenment) was reflected in Carlyle's powerful assertion in his 1837 book, *Sartor Resartus*.

Stands he [man] not thereby in the centre of Immensities, in the complex of Eternities? He feels; power has been given to him to know, to believe; nay does not the spirit of Love, free in its celestial primeval brightness, even here, though but for moments, look through?

(quoted in Turner, 2014, p. 233)

Hence, conclusions, contrasting with and quite separate from those of a materialist philosophical outlook, were drawn from 'the reasons of the heart' of Pascal, or from the spiritual dimension of 'man' as portrayed by Carlyle, or from the 'sense of sublime something' of Wordsworth, or from the 'continual perception of Sanctity in the whole of nature' by Ruskin.

The idea of the Holy

Thus Otto (1923/1958) points to, and endeavours to articulate, this sense of what he refers to as the 'numinous', or 'the holy', as a category of interpretation peculiar to the sphere of religious writing and practising. There is, indeed, the paradox in its prevalence across cultures and ages (albeit in different attempts to articulate and manifest it), whilst at the same time in the failure to define it clearly. The 'numinous' seems unavoidable, and yet eludes apprehension in terms of our normal concepts. After all, the words we use in pursuit of understanding are inescapably drawn from our experience of the material world, thereby showing their inadequacy for grasping the 'numinous'. To repeat again the words of William James (1902, p. 58) in his *Varieties of Religious Experience*,

it is as if there were in the human consciousness *a sense of reality, a feeling of objective presence, a perception* of what we may well call '*something there*', more

> deep and more general than any of the special and particular 'senses' by which the current psychology supposes existing reality to be originally revealed.
>
> *(italics are James' own)*

Therefore, Otto (p. 7) concludes that the central religious idea of 'the holy' (a primary datum of consciousness)

> cannot, strictly speaking, be taught, it can only be evoked, awakened in the mind; as everything that 'comes of the spirit' must be awakened.

And that evocation comes in many ways and from many sources.

> Let us follow it up with every effort of sympathy and imaginative intuition wherever it is to be found, in the lives of those around us, in sudden, strong ebullitions of personal piety and the frames of mind such ebullitions evince, in the fixed and ordered solemnities of rites and liturgies, and again in the atmosphere that clings to the old religious monuments and buildings, to temples and churches. If we do so, we shall find we are dealing with something for which there is only one appropriate expression, *mysterium tremendum*.
>
> *(p. 12)*

Inevitably attempts are made to articulate this 'mysterium', thereby bringing reason to bear upon the 'non-rational', through use of metaphor and analogy, applying concepts which prevail in human life but which can never fully comprehend the 'numinous' (concepts such as 'creator', 'omnipotent', 'omniscient').

In developing this theme, Otto (p. 48) uses the analogy of musical appreciation.

> Music, in short, arouses in us an experience and vibrations of mood that are quite specific in kind and must simply be called 'musical', but the ... manifold variations of this experience exhibit – though again only in part – definite, if fugitive, analogies and correspondences with our ordinary non-musical emotional states, and so can call these into consciousness and blend with them.

Here then we see, analogous to the search for understanding 'the numinous', the attempt to articulate in this case the experience of music which is *sui genesis*. In so doing, reason is brought to bear upon the non-rational (not the 'irrational'), though never quite comprehending it. But that 'non-rational' is partly captured in the enactment of religious rituals, in the Muslims' call to prayer, in the sublimity of gothic architecture, in sublime pieces of music, in so many great works of art, but also in the deep feeling of guilt for wrongs done – an aspect to be developed further in Chapter 5.

The French sociologist Emile Durkheim, in his book *Moral Education* (1961, p. 3), had argued for purely secular education; nonetheless, in his later book, *Elementary*

Forms of Religious Life, he wrote (as paraphrased by Grace, 2016, p. 1) of the distinctive understanding of human development and of its religious dimension which concerned that which is

> sacred – superior in dignity and power to the elements of mundane life, to things 'set apart', to concepts of the transcendent and divine, of souls and spirits, and to the ultimate destiny of persons. The sacred is holy, ineffable and mysterious.

Having a faith, therefore, is to have a strong sense of a reality which transcends the phenomenal world but which has been articulated and made manifest over time in ways of life, in rituals, in the arts, but always subject to refinement in the light of further experience, others' lives, dialogue and philosophical critique.

It should be noted at this stage, most importantly for the 'challenges for religious education' which are concluded in the penultimate chapter of this book, that such 'feeling experiences' (such 'consciousness') have become the subject of systematic research into the experiences of many people by the Religious Experience Research Unit at the University of Oxford, in the tradition of William James. These include the experiences of children, as reflected in Robinson's (1977), *The Original Vision, a Study of the Religious Experiences of Childhood*, and in Priestley's (1985) 'Towards finding the hidden curriculum: a consideration of the spiritual dimension of experience in curriculum planning', which was referred to in Chapter 1. Clearly the implications of such research create yet a further 'challenge for religious education', as will be explained in the penultimate chapter.

In all this, one sees the struggle between, on the one hand, the 'non-rational', and, on the other hand, the 'rational' attempts to articulate the sacred or numinous, though never fully doing so. It surely is a case (to refer again to 5th-century philosopher Boethius) of philosophy being the 'lady handmaiden of theology', the significance of which will be dwelt upon more fully in Chapter 4. But the struggle between the 'non-rational' and the 'rational' was well expressed in Plato's Timaeas, quoted by Otto (p. 95):

> Therefore is it an impossible task both to discover the creator and the father of this whole universe and to publish the discovery of him in words for all to understand.

The rational and the non-rational

One needs to note, on the one hand, the assumed 'rational' connection seen by many between 'belief' and 'feeling' (that is, the consciousness which is embedded in strong feelings, as reflected in Pascal, Otto, Ruskin, James or Carlyle), but, on the other hand, the denial, inherited particularly from the Enlightenment, of any such rational connection with what appears to be the 'non-rational'.

28 Faith

The interim conclusion, therefore, that we seem to have reached so far is that

(i) the central focus of religious faith is on the existence and the nature of a Being we call 'God';
(ii) God is not knowable in the normal understanding of 'knowing something', (namely, via ultimate verification through sense experience); and therefore the concepts through which we describe sensible reality seem inadequate for understanding that God;
(iii) nonetheless, through non-rational experience and awareness (what might be referred to as a 'phenomenological consciousness', or, according to Pascal, the 'reasons of the heart'), we are often, or can be made, aware of a transcendent reality, the numinous, which many identify with 'God';
(iv) therefore, within the evolving nature of religious education, as explained in Chapter 1, connections can be made between the interests and consciousness of young people and the idea of the sacred or the holy as described in the accounts given by William James, Pascal or Otto;
(v) however, from a particular philosophical position, such a rational connection cannot be made between 'believing' and 'feelings', as described by Pascal's 'reasons of the heart', or by Otto's 'idea of the holy', or by Ruskin's 'continual perception of sanctity in the whole of nature', or by Carlyle's 'spirit of Love, free in its celestial primeval brightness';
(vi) nonetheless, reason, partly through philosophical clarification, seeks to articulate the significance and meaning of such experiences and insights in capturing their essential features and the arguments for justifying the beliefs which underlie them (for example, through use of analogy, which shall be explained in Chapter 4). And the significance of this will be raised in the 'Challenges for Religious Education' in Chapter 9.

Rationality

To pursue this argument further, it is useful to explain a little more about what I mean by reason and rationality. Rationality lies in providing the evidence for promoting a particular belief or set of beliefs. But in most cases of everyday living, the evidence, though the best we can muster, cannot guarantee the conclusion. For example, the back light on my bicycle cannot be trusted – it keeps fading. It is rational to think that it needs new batteries, so I put in new batteries. It still fails to work. Another solution is tried. Hence, what normally would be regarded as good evidence may prove to be wrong. 'Evidence' does not entail correct conclusions, let alone certainty, but it can be strong as well as weak. And it becomes stronger when seemingly confirmed by other strands of evidence. Thus, back to Pascal, (quoted in Cottingham, 2014, p. 15) 'it is our heart that senses God, not our reason', and thus 'we know the truth, not only by reason, but also by the heart'.

In his book, *What is Faith?,* Anthony Kenny reflects on the two extremes of belief: on the one hand, 'credulity' where beliefs are held on little or no appropriate evidence related to that sort of belief; on the opposite hand, 'scepticism' where there is a refusal to entertain any sort of evidence. The 'mean', to use Aristotle's concept of virtue (here the theological virtue of faith), lies in between the two extremes. It is a question, therefore, of

> whether the evidence for the existence of God is sufficient to *warrant* the degree of assent characteristic of the believer.
> *(Kenny, 1992, p. 8, but this author's italics)*

Of course, such an intellectual virtue applies equally to those who conclude the non-existence of God, but also whose scepticism may be at the other extreme from the credulity of which those with faith are accused of being guilty.

However, the concept of 'warrant' employed by Kenny, especially in his reference to Platinga's (1979) paper, 'Is belief in God rational?', is important. In so many, if not most, circumstances in life, we reach, and must reach, conclusions which are 'warranted' by the evidence, where such evidence may have different strands. Not one of the strands by itself 'warrants' the conclusion and basis for belief, but many strands may converge such that together they *warrant* belief – short though they may be of 'logical proof'. The prevalence of religious faith from the earliest times, subject to constant critique and refinement and arising for many believers from the 'reasons of the heart', as reflected in the previous section, would absolve the believer from the intellectual vice of 'credulity', even though it would be compatible with shades of doubt which stimulated further thought, further reference to argument and evidence and further involvement in the long tradition of philosophical thinking about the existence of God (see Chapter 6 of this book on the different shades of doubt). But that tradition of critical thinking and then of personal assent (itself open to much refinement) would be constantly enhanced by a 'collection of premises' describing different experiences and arguments which together strongly suggest substantial support. Thus, as Kenny argues (pp. 25–27), the initial reason for believing may not be the reason for continuing to believe. On the other hand, the further premises of a different kind, though not by themselves conclusive, would together with other arguments re-enforce the earlier (though weakly held) beliefs.

A way of life

There is a danger in so focusing (if not exclusively) upon the reasonableness of a belief to forget that such reasonableness cannot escape how having such a belief is embodied in a way of life, in seeing one's responsibilities in a particular way, in relating differently to others and in acknowledging God through prayer. Just as 'knowing that' is implicit in 'knowing how', so 'having a belief' is implicit in 'a way of behaving' even where such a belief may not be clearly articulated.

Richard Swinburne (1981) begins his book *Faith and Reason* by warning against a purely propositional account of belief (that is 'one believes that') and by emphasising belief as embodied in action and ways of living (that is 'one believes practically'), stimulated perhaps in the practical manifestation of that belief in prayer and liturgy. Thus, later in the book (p. 91), he quotes Pascal, where the believer helps the unbeliever by suggesting he 'acts as if'

> You want to be cured of unbelief and you ask for the remedy; learn from those who were once bound like you. . . . They behaved just as if they did believe, taking holy water, having masses said, and so on. That will make you believe quite naturally.

Thus, in making the sign of the cross or in genuflecting before the Blessed Sacrament, there is in one's action the implicit belief of God's presence – a belief which becomes more explicit when it is reflected on over time.

Therefore, whatever the 'reasons of the heart' which stimulated an initial, though faltering, belief, those reasons may have introduced the neophyte to a way of life, to rituals and to interpretations of experience (and thus to a 'faith') which provide further insights and a grander and deeper understanding of life, as that is captured in a more comprehensive belief system.

Interim conclusion

It is important, therefore, at this stage of the argument to summarise what we mean by 'having a faith', whilst recognising that more needs to be said to clarify the place of reason in adhering to that faith and thereby to anticipate the objections of those for whom such beliefs are seen to be irrational and for whom therefore the teaching of them in school cannot be justified, amounting possibly to indoctrination.

So far, there has been an articulation of what 'faith' means to many people, namely, a sense of the 'numinous' and a way of life, which is manifest in rituals, moral direction and the spiritual life, as described in Chapter 1, though not on a rational basis in the sense of proof or truth criteria for such beliefs, even though reasons are given which, in the words of Newman, 'warrant assent' – an assent which is fortified by the *experience* of a religious form of life (see Newman, 1870/1955). To repeat the earlier reference to William James (encapsulating what was recognised by Pascal, Otto and others), it is

> as if there were in human *consciousness* a sense of reality, a feeling of objective presence, a perception of what we might call 'something there'.

It is to this central issue we must now turn:

- first, in the following chapter (Chapter 3), to the philosophical basis for claiming the truth of such a belief in God, countering the claims of those who, given a particular view of 'truth' and verification, would seem to undermine any rational basis for claiming religious knowledge (and thereby religious education);

- second, however, within such a philosophical account (given also the role of the *phenomenon* of 'consciousness' in the experience which gives rise to the assent to there being God, as argued by Pascal or James or Otto), to the insights given within the philosophical tradition of 'phenomenology'. As we saw in Chapter 1, a phenomenological approach was seen to be one way of reconciling religious education within a broader liberal and secular context, thereby creating a reason for and justification of religious education.

Then, however, in Chapter 4, it will be necessary to fathom the deeper understanding of this 'hidden God', which constitutes that faith and, for the most part but not exclusively, made available (so it is claimed) through revelation. For we still seem to be left with the problem concerning the possible knowledge, not so much of there being a God, but rather of the nature of that God such that He can be the focus of our lives – entering into the spiritual life which characterises a 'faith'. 'Transcendence' would seem to indicate that the divine exceeds all limits of human understanding. Hark back to the statement of Aquinas, that we may know *that* God is, but not *what* He is. The 'numinous' seems to escape meaningful description. But if that is so, if we cannot know anything about the 'mysterium tremendum', then it would seem hardly to be the focus and inspiration of a religious form of life – that is of a 'faith' – and thus of religious formation and education.

Bibliography

Boethius, 5th Century, *De Consolatione Philosophiae.*
Carlyle, 1837, *Sartor Resartus*, ed. Hudson, W.D., London: Dent.
Cottingham, J., 2009, *Why Believe*, London: Continuum.
Cottingham, J., 2014, *Philosophy of Religion*, Cambridge University Press.
Dawkins, R., 2006, *The God Delusion*, London: Bantam Press.
Durkheim, E., 1961, *Moral Education: A Study in the Theory and Application of the Sociology of Education*, New York: The Free Press.
Durkheim, E., 1971, *Elementary Forms of the Religious Life*, London: Allen and Unwin.
Grace, G., 2016, *Faith, Mission and Challenge in Catholic Education*, London: Routledge.
Hewer, C.T.R., 2006, *Understanding Islam*, London: SCM Press.
James, W., 1902, *Varieties of Religious Experience*, London: Gifford Lectures.
Kenny, A., 1992, *What is Faith?* Oxford: Oxford University Press.
Kierkegaard, 1844, *Philosophical Fragments.*
Lonergan, B., 1957, *Insight*, London: Longmans.
NCC (National Curriculum Council) Report, 1993, *Spiritual and Moral Development*, London: HMSO.
Newman, J.H., 1844, *University Sermons*, Oxford: Oxford University Press.
Newman, J.H., 1870/1955, *A Grammar of Assent*, Image Books.
Otto, R., 1923/1958, *The Idea of the Holy*, Oxford: Oxford University Press.
Pascal, E., 1670, *Pensees*, ed., Krailsheimer, A.J., Harmondsworth: Penguin.
Platinga, A., 1979, 'Is belief in god rational?' in Delaney, C.F., ed., *Rationality and Religious Belief*, Notre Dame: University of Notre Dame Press.
Priestley, J., 1985, 'Towards finding the original curriculum: A consideration of the spiritual dimension of experience in curriculum planning', *British Journal of Religious Education*, 7 (3).

Robinson, E., 1977, *The Original Vision: A Study of the Religious Experience of Childhood*, Oxford: Manchester College.
Sacks, J., 1997, *The Politics of Hope*, London: Jonathan Cope.
Spens Report, 1938, *Secondary Education with Special Reference to Grammar Schools and Technical High Schools*, London: Board of Education.
Swinburne, R., 1981, *Faith and Reason*, Oxford: Clarendon Press.
Turner, F.M., 2014, *European Intellectual History from Rousseau to Nietzsche*, Yale University Press.

3
BELIEF IN GOD
Knowledge, evidence and assent

The book continues, therefore, with an examination of what counts as making sense of the 'numinous'. It thereby provides a more detailed epistemological examination arising from the claims of the 'reasonableness' for believing in God, as reflected in the last chapter. It does so by examining what counts as knowledge and its foundations (which looks as if it has been dodged in the foregoing account), looking critically at those who, in the spirit of the Enlightenment, would deny there to be such a philosophical basis. This requires some examination, not only of more recent theories of knowledge (in particular those arising from the Enlightenment), but also of 'metaphysics' as a way of knowing. The chapter therefore resurrects Aristotelian, Thomist and Islamic philosophical traditions, arguing for the reasonableness of 'real assent' (as opposed to mere 'notional assent') to belief in God.

The problem: religious education and truth claims

Chapter 1 reflected the growing reluctance to promote religious education where such education assumed the truth of religious claims – the truth, for example, of the claim that there is a God, and that God revealed or disclosed Himself in the person of Jesus Christ or through the prophet Mohammad or in the visions of Moses and the prophets. Indeed, as we have seen, there is reluctance to talk about 'truth', choosing instead to recognise the need merely to understand what religious people believe within their different cultural communities. Such understanding 'from the outside', as it were, frees one from consideration of the truth of one's respective beliefs. That would increasingly seem to be the case with religious education within the 'common school' (open to all faiths and none).

However, Wright (2007, p. 196 sq) insists that religious education should deal with questions of truth 'with a capital T', which is to be found

> not in individual experiences but in the public linguistic traditions and communities that uphold these truth-claims and make them alive for their adherents.

There are, in other words, philosophical and theological traditions which have developed (openly, critically and systematically within long-standing communities) claims to religious truth which become the bases of forms of life. Such traditions are inherited, yet constantly open to development. Certainly the continued existence of 'Faith Schools' within such 'public linguistic traditions', whether inside or outside of the State system, must raise the issues about the truth of their respective religious beliefs. Thus, according to Hubery, 1972, in his book, *Christian Education in State and Church*,

> Christian education was about the search for truth and about discovery, not evangelism.
>
> *(quoted in Cooling, 1994, p. 96)*

What sense, therefore, can be given to the notion 'search for truth' in matters of religion? And how far should the claims for such 'truth' be the basis of religious education, as it is in other subjects like science and mathematics — and indeed 'history', which raises similar problems about the truth of the claims being made?

The answer to such questions is not easy, partly because there is no universal philosophical agreement upon what is meant by 'the truth'.

Knowledge, truth and verification

A common analysis of what we mean by 'truth' is that it is a quality of those statements about the world which 'correspond' correctly to the reality they are describing — the 'correspondence theory of truth'. Thus, for example, the statement, 'John got wet on his way to school', is true if 'John' (correctly pointing to a person in the 'real world') was in fact on his way to school and got wet — given the agreed meaning within our language of such words as 'wet' and 'school'. There is a one-to-one relationship between 'word', within a shared language, and 'object', which exists independently of my observations. Hence, in pursuit of 'the truth', one seeks *verification* of the statement through empirical evidence — what one sees, hears, feels or smells.

Such a correspondence theory of truth was clearly stated by Professor A.J. Ayer (1936) in *Language, Truth and Logic,* according to which there are only two kinds of meaningful statements, namely, those which can be empirically verified through the senses and those which are reducible to logical proof (as in mathematics). All other so-called truth claims are meaningless since they lack any such mode of verification. Hence, religious statements sit alongside moral and aesthetic statements in being unverifiable and thereby meaningless, unless one extends the concept of 'meaning' more broadly to the *use* of words, in this case to the capacity of such 'statements' to produce some sort of distinctive feeling. With regard to moral statements, this was referred to as 'the emotive theory of ethics' (see Ayer, op.cit. ch.6). They are but the expression of emotions, but made to appear like factual claims.

There are clearly difficulties in such a restrictive theory of truth and verification.

First, the most obvious difficulty is the statement of the theory itself, for that statement can be seen to be true neither by empirical investigation nor by pure logic. The theory itself must be meaningless.

Second, however, although such a correspondence theory of truth seems plausible for many claims which are made, what counts as 'verification' of those claims is not so clear. Take, for example. the statement 'Mark believes in God'. It is not clear what empirical observations verify such a statement (that is, the *claimed fact* that Mark so believes). One might point to the fact that he says his prayers or goes to church, but such observations verify only propositions about what can be seen, not about his thoughts, meditations or beliefs. What is observed may well provide *evidence* for the truth of the statements about belief, but it is logically possible that in fact he may be deceiving, or merely pleasing, his family. One cannot directly observe intentions, feelings or mental acts. Similarly, for example, the observable act of one's hand being raised could be interpreted as 'stretching', 'waving goodbye' or 'seeking attention'. Interpretation of what is observed requires a more complete background account of the circumstances in which the observable behaviour occurs, including possibly the actor's own account (or 'disclosures') of intentions and motives. It can never be certain whether that which is observed might not have been misinterpreted. Lack of certainty is by no means confined to religious claims to the truth.

Third, what is observed is necessarily interpreted within the concepts through which the observations are made sense of, and such concepts belong to wider conceptual frameworks which are constantly being acquired through intercourse with other people and cultures. People from different cultures may see 'the same thing' very differently. The visual image, for example, is interpreted within a framework of ideas or concepts, which may be strange to someone from outside that cultural group. Therefore, critical of a 'correspondence theory of knowledge' is what has been called a 'coherence theory of knowledge', where the description of the world arises as much from the conceptual framework which is logically coherent, which is socially inherited (and constantly evolving) and which seems 'to work' (that is, enables one to anticipate the consequences of one's actions within the world, howsoever that is conceived).

Fourth, in the world of 'post-modernism' (see below, p. 36, as to what is referred to as 'modernism'), the prevalence of different ways of conceptualising experience is taken further to an assault on the very notion of objectively true and justified beliefs, as exemplified particularly in the arguments of Lyotard's (1984), *The Post-Modern Condition: a report on knowledge*. This is reflected in the accusation that any reports which do not fit in with one's ways of seeing things are but 'fake news'. What is claimed to be true is the construction or re-construction of reality to meet the idea of the reality for which one wishes. Any restraints on what one wishes to believe are rejected by the critic as alternative reconstructions of reality. 'Facts' are not discovered but created (derived from the Latin word 'facere', to make). Hence, religious beliefs are but the shared social conceptions of the world by particular religious associations through which religious 'reality' is created. There is no stepping outside such a way of conceiving reality to check whether or not it is reasonable.

One must, of course, be careful against the errors of this form of idealism, which enters into philosophical thinking – and turning up in the sociology of knowledge, as witnessed in the influential book edited by M.F.D. Young (1972), *Knowledge and Control*, which delivered the message that how we see the world depends on those who, being in positions of power, determine how that world is 'constructed'. Different people or groups of people may well 'see' things differently because of the different ideas through which they interpret experience, shaped by those who are in positions of influence.

There is, of course, an important element of truth in this. The nuclear physicist will see a physical phenomenon differently from one who has no knowledge of physics. But it does not follow from such an understanding that different conceptual accounts are all equally acceptable. There is a reality independent of our conceiving it, and such conceptions need constantly to be adapted, even rejected, because of further experience. Once again with reference to Aquinas, *objective quoad id quod concipitur, non autem quoad modem quo concipitur* – 'objective as far as that which is conceived, not as far as the mode of conceiving it'. There is a reality 'out there', independent of our conceiving it, which restricts what might be an appropriate account of it. But nonetheless, there can be different and rival accounts of that reality, always open to reformulation in the light of criticism and experience.

However, one must recognise the pull of scientific procedures as the paradigm of rational enquiry. The exponents of the principle of verification, referred to above, as a criterion of meaningful propositions, may have been mistaken in putting this forward as a comprehensive theory of meaning (thereby relegating religious claims to the class of the 'meaningless', along with many other kinds of statements, such as moral and aesthetic), but they did provide clarity on what counts as an understanding of experience of the physical world, which has lessons for the meanings of religious statements. Thus, it was argued that the meaning of a statement entails recognition of the means by which such a statement can be judged to be true (or false). It is important to explain this a little further.

Modernity: science as a paradigm of knowledge

From the time depicted as that of the 'age of enlightenment', expressed by Immanuel Kant (1784) as

> man's release from his self-tutelage. Tutelage is man's inability to make use of his understanding without direction from another. Self-incurred is this tutelage when its cause lies not in lack of reason but in lack of resolution and courage to use it without direction from another. *Sapere aude!* 'Have courage to use your own reason' that is the motto of enlightenment.

Thus the 'enlightenment' indicated an emphasis on the use of reason, inspired by advances in science and freed from the role and authority of religion and its institutions. There would be a liberation from authority in the pursuit of the truth. Such a view spread quickly through Western Europe, led by *les philosophes* in France, in the light of the progress of science – the scientific outlook and method.

In Britain, this was clearly expressed by John Locke (1693) in his *Third Letter on Toleration*.

> How well-grounded and great soever the assurance of faith may be wherewith it is received; but faith it is still and not knowledge; persuasion and not certainty. This is the highest the nature of things will permit us to go in matters of revealed religion which are therefore called matters of faith; a persuasion of our own minds, short of knowledge, is the result that determines us in such truths.

Hence, there is seen to be a sharp contrast between 'faith' and 'knowledge' which is based on reason.

David Hume (1748, p. XII, part 3) continued within the same empiricist tradition, arguing that conclusions drawn from any basis other than purely logical premises (as in mathematics), or from what can be sensibly observed (as in science), should be 'committed to the flames for it can contain nothing but sophistry'.

Therefore, the growth and success of science came to be seen as the paradigm of knowledge, whether that be knowledge of the physical world or indeed of the psychological world, which itself was seen to be reducible to what can be understood in the language of the natural sciences, as reflected in educational research in the theory of 'behaviour modification' (see Gurney, 1981). Such scientific understanding requires systematic observation of the physical world – what ultimately can be witnessed and checked by sensible experience. In the light of experience, one can hypothesise what will happen in certain conditions and as a result of certain preceding or causal activities. Thus are built-up bodies of verifiable statements which constitute models or theories as to how things work in the physical world and which provide the basis for further predictions.

Furthermore, from such a position there has emerged a common commitment amongst influential scientists to a 'New Atheism', as reflected in several publications, for instance: Harris, 2004, *The End of Faith: Religion, Terror, and the Future of Reason*; Dawkins, 2006, *The God Delusion*; Hitchins, 2007, *God is not Great* – dramatically sub-titled 'how religion poisons everything'.

However, harking back to what was said in the previous section about conceptual schemes or models or theories failing to predict correctly, such models or schemes need constantly to be revised or even, in extreme cases, rejected. Within science, there can be no absolute certainty. Thus, as Popper (1972, p. 34) argued, scientific knowledge grows through criticism. And therefore, as stated by Harlen (2010, p. 23, quoted in Stern, 2018, p. 2) in relation to the teaching of science,

> A scientific theory or model representing relationships between variables or components of a system must fit the observations available at the time and lead to predictions that can be tested. Any theory or model is provisional and

subject to revision in the light of new data even though it may have led to predictions in accord with data in the past. Every model has its strengths and limitations in accounting for observations.

Therefore, what might thus be seen as a complete divide between scientific and religious claims to knowledge may not be so extreme as often thought. Karl Popper (2002, pp. 170–171) goes so far as to say,

> My thesis is that what we call 'science' is differentiated from the older myths, not by being something distinct from a myth, but by being accompanied by a second-order tradition – that of critically discussing the myth. . . . If we understand that, then . . . we shall understand that, in a certain sense, science is myth-making just as religion is.

It is not surprising, therefore, that so many renowned scientists do not see the massive gulf between religious and scientific explanations of the universe, as often supposed. Jon Lennox (2009) points to the 'towering figures of science' (Kepler, Pascal, Boyle, Newton, Babbage, Mendel, Pasteur and Clark Maxwell) for whom scientific and religious understanding are seen to be in harmonious agreement. Lennox (p. 8) quotes Johannes Kepler, thus:

> The chief aim of all explanations of the world would be to discover the rational order which has been imposed on it by God, and which he revealed to us in the language of mathematics.

Indeed, as the three scientists and philosophers (Briggs, A., Halvorson, H. and Steane, A.) argue in their recent book, *It Keeps Me Seeking* (p. 8):

> The natural world has mathematical harmony built into it at a deep level. This is quite striking and may give one pause for thought. . . . We (the authors) think that the emergence of life and death, and love and hate, on planet earth suggests that the universe is freighted with meaning . . . in somewhat the same way that a written text is freighted with meaning. This rich process is not just a line of tumbling dominoes, nor a whirlwind, but a story, a narrative.

However, it may well be that, whereas science is seeking to explain how things in the material world happen (what counts as 'knowledge', although always tentative and open to further testing and criticism), religious accounts would not claim to be 'on the same playing field' or in competition. Anthony Kenny (1992, p. 112), in his book, *What is Faith?*, argues,

> The way in which God accounts for the unexplained is not by figuring in some further explanation. When we invoke God we do not explain the world, or any series of phenomena in the world. The mode of intelligibility

which is provided by the invocation of God is something of quite different kind.... The concept of God provides not explanation but understanding.

By way of interim conclusion, therefore, one might argue that, although the advance of scientific enquiry influenced the development of an 'enlightened theory of meaning', which in turn led to the exclusion of religious statements as meaningless, such a theory of meaning did but enlighten the difference between empirical statements and other lines of enquiry. The verification principle expounded by Ayer could not, and should not, be equally applied to all other statements, including religious ones.

However, there is a lesson to be learnt, as already stated, namely, that to understand the meaning of a statement is to recognise the sort of evidence which makes such a statement reasonable to consider, to take seriously, to give assent to and to act upon accordingly. The 'truths of religion' cannot get away from a 'principle of verification of some sort' whereby such statements are seen to be distinctively meaningful and defensible. It is this which is addressed in the phenomenological account of religious experience referred to in Chapter 1 and which we need now to examine from a more philosophical perspective.

The phenomenological account of knowledge

Constant reference has been made, especially in Chapter 2, to the kinds of *consciousness* attained through what Pascal referred to (through 'reasons of the heart') as a 'Being Who transcends experience', or through that awareness of what Otto referred to as the 'numinous', and exemplified through the many examples given by William James in his *Varieties of Religious Experience*. It is the constant reference to this distinctive 'consciousness' (this 'phenomenon', difficult though it is to make sense of), which underlies what is referred to as the phenomenological awareness within religious claims and which has shaped religious education, as reflected in Chapters 1 and 2, in that it transcends specific religious beliefs and opens the mind to the possibility of religious faith and discourse. Indeed, as Gearon (2014, p. 100) clearly shows in the chapter, 'Phenomenology and religious education', phenomenology

> would provide the grounds for a 'neutral' study of religion ... a highly suitable approach for those socio-political and educational contexts which confront religious plurality.

Thus, what might be referred to at this stage as 'subjective experience' became the object of interest to a philosophical tradition of enquiry which is referred to as 'phenomenology'. There is a need, so it was argued by the 19th-century philosopher Brentano (1874), to distinguish between the act of consciousness itself (the psychic phenomenon) and the object which one is conscious of but which is given meaning through the subjective 'intention'. Here 'intention' refers to the activity of the mind shaped by its *a priori* structure, by previous ideas, by emotions such as pleasure and fear, and by the agent's purposes. How one sees the world is determined not solely by the exterior world itself. It is this mental structure and consciousness themselves which are the object of phenomenological study. Such consciousness is 'intentional' in the sense that it 'points out' and thereby shapes the world which is external to the conscious subject. One cannot escape from this 'subjectivity'. And here we can see the influence of Kant's exposition of the *a priori* conditions for rational thought, whether about the physical world or about moral duty – the phenomenology of the fundamental structure of consciousness.

This provides a philosophical background to the religious education programmes, referred to in Chapter 1 (and developed by Professor Ninian Smart, 1968), which focus upon the 'phenomenon', the initial consciousness, which can point to (though not conclusively) an experience of 'the sacred' – a deeper and broader account of experience than is revealed in science, and the possibility of a 'transcendent being' reflecting the awareness of the sacred, of the holy, of the 'mysterium tremendum'.

It is this 'consciousness to be opened up' which, as argued in Chapter 8, is one of the 'challenges' for religious education in schools.

Such an account, therefore, would be seen as a criticism of the empiricism which assumed a comprehensive understanding of 'knowledge, truth and certainty', as recounted above. That failed to recognise the mental structure of what Edmund Husserl (in his influential work, *Phenomenological Method and Phenomenological Philosophy*, 1922, and the inheritor of Brentano's philosophy) referred to as the 'a priori' structure of the mind which shaped the meaning we attach to external experience. Looking at consciousness itself, one can focus on the idea or the meaning of 'the self', of 'moral value' (see Chapter 5 of this book), of 'the sacred', even of 'external objects', through which we give sense to experience – the *a priori* shaping of experience whether or not that be of an external and physical world.

In so doing, phenomenology would take seriously the different ways in which this consciousness is opened up – through art and music, through silent contemplation, through the psychological sciences, or through the experience of liturgy and ritual, all of which attempt to express a consciousness which cannot easily be put into words. It is this 'consciousness to be opened up' which, as argued in Chapter 9, is one of the 'challenges' for religious education in schools.

Such a philosophical study, or analysis, of consciousness itself, requires a 'bracketing off' ('epoche') of the ontological basis of the experience, that is, the independent reality of that of which one is conscious. Thus, phenomenology, as a philosophical position, is not easy to articulate, but its influence was strong, especially on the continent of Europe, as reflected in the work of Heidegger who, in *Being and Time* (1927), argued that western philosophy had forgotten the 'Being', the superior Being in the hierarchy of beings, and immersed itself in the study of 'beings'. For Heidegger, phenomenology was the ontological analysis of man as a 'being' who is able to raise the question of, and then is open to, 'Being as such'. Philosophy, therefore, would be seen as the pursuit of the task of converting man's unreflective and implicit apprehension of Being into systematic and explicit knowledge. This might be seen no doubt as a return to metaphysics as a form of knowledge, once thought to have been killed off.

But has *meta*physics – the systematic study of what transcends 'physics' (namely, the empirical world, understood through science) – been killed off? Can there not be the reasoning which leads from the world of finite beings to the existence of an infinite Being, from a world of contingent causal relations to one of a necessary and uncaused Cause – thereby giving a more defined account of Otto's 'idea of the holy' or of Pascal's 'reasons of the heart', or of the 'numinous' of William James, as these are explained in Chapter 2?

As Kant states in the opening words of the *Critique of Pure Reason,*

> That all our knowledge begins with experience, there can be no doubt. . . . But although all our knowledge begins with experience, it by no means follows that all arises out of experience.

Metaphysical knowledge: further arguments for God's existence?

However, has metaphysical knowledge been 'killed off, as was thought?

There is a tradition of such 'metaphysical thinking' from Aristotle onwards which, given its persistence in both Christian and Islamic philosophical thought, needs to be taken seriously. In *Metaphysics* (p. 363), Aristotle argues,

> The material generation of one thing from another cannot go on *ad infinitum* . . . nor can the efficient causes form an endless series. . . . Similarly, the final cause cannot recede to infinity – walking for the sake of health, health for the sake of happiness, happiness for the sake of something else. . . . But of series which are infinite in this way, and of the infinite in general, all the terms, down to and excluding the present, are equally intermediate. Thus if there is no first term there is no cause at all.

Aristotle adds (p. 365),

> If the kinds of cause were infinite in number, knowledge would be equally impossible; for we think we know a thing only when we have ascertained all its causes, but what is additively infinite cannot be traversed by thought in a finite time.

Much of the *Metaphysics*, therefore, consists of working through the details of such insights into the different sorts of causality (material, efficient, final and formal), showing how there must be a termination in the explanatory chain of 'finite beings' in an uncaused cause, namely, 'Being qua Being'.

It is this Aristotelian philosophical landscape, which was taken up within Islam, particularly Al-Farabi (10th century), Avicenna (11th century) and Averroes (12th century), although Al Gazali (11th century), in his *Incoherence of the Philosophers*, aimed at taming the Hellenistic trend in Islamic thought. Nonetheless, that philosophical tradition sought

> a bridgehead of reason between eternal principles and truths of religion and contemporary, contingent realities of the world, working within the broad, consensually accepted parameters of traditional Islamic doctrine.
>
> *(Wilkinson, 2015, p. 10)*

Similarly, the Aristotelian philosophy entered the scholastic tradition, as pioneered by Aquinas in the 13th century – but interacted with the Islamic Averroes/Aristotelian tradition which prevailed at the University of Paris around 1270. It is important, in anticipation of Chapter 9 and the challenge to religious education in our schools, to be aware of the close interaction between the Islamic and Christian philosophers (and also Jewish, with special reference to Maimonides in the 12th century) in addressing the relation between faith in God and the rational basis for that faith, building on the unifying foundations of Aristotle in particular. There is much in common here which is highly relevant to the development of religious education within a multi-ethnic and multi-cultural society.

What, therefore, sets the theist going is the search for further intelligibility of the world of finite things and contingent relationships, that is, the world as understood within science. But such intelligibility, so the theist argues, cannot be found in an infinite chain of causes. That is why, as MacIntyre (2009, p. 77), argues:

> Scientific enquiry always involves trying to move beyond our present explanations, yet never can reach a point where the phenomena which it studies have been made finally intelligible.

Such a point would be reached by the existence of a cause which did not itself require a further cause,

> its existence and nature requiring no further explanation . . . a being whose essence and existence are identical
>
> *(MacIntyre, op.cit.)*

Hence, it is important to understand different ways in which, in affirming such causality, the concept of cause has been invoked. Two such ways may be summarised as follows.

Proof from efficient causality

In so arguing, MacIntyre is writing within that Aristotelian tradition upon which the Islamic and Christian philosophers drew in the early and late Middle Ages. St. Thomas Aquinas, in both *Summa Theologica* and *Summa Contra Gentiles* (but also drawing upon Avicenna's notion of 'efficient cause'), argued that any proof must begin with the sensible experience of the world of finite and contingent beings.

But such a world is constituted of things which interact causally on each other, one thing moving another or one thing having been given the power (*potential*) of self-motion. Either way, movement or efficient causality (as distinct from final causality – see below) in the world of finite and mobile objects requires an explanation by reference to prior moving objects or to prior bestowal of the potency to move. But, in keeping with Aristotle's analysis, such a chain of causality cannot go back infinitely; otherwise it would never get started. Hence, there needs to be a first mover, a first cause, and that we call God.

It may be objected, in the light of what has been said about the nature of causality as described in the section on 'science as paradigm of knowledge', that we are wrongly trading on the use of a concept beyond the empirical context in which it has meaning. Is this not a case of what Wittgenstein (1958, pp. 1, 109) referred to as 'the bewitchment of the intelligence by the misuse of words' – moving from 'effect', as understood within the context of the empirical world, to 'cause' which, by its *claimed* nature, is here seen to be external to that empirical world? The response to such an objection would be that words have meaning when applied analogously; there are sufficient similarities within different contexts for the same word to be applied without the word being applied equivocally.

Nonetheless, one can appreciate the difficulties which many must feel in such an argument, pushing as it does along a causal chain to a First Cause, the nature of whom must necessarily be 'to be', and whose very essence, therefore, is that of 'being', and thus referred to as Being qua Being (see Gilson, 1961). One can see how readers may balk at such a designation of the 'First Cause', so abstract and apparently using 'being' as a predicate. And yet the problem raised by Aristotle remains, such that it seems reasonable, even if mysterious, to think about the possibility of a 'First Cause'.

Indeed, similar reasoning constantly re-appears in philosophy. As pointed out, though questioned, by Swinburne (2004, pp. 148 *sq.*), Leibniz, in his work, *On the Ultimate Origination of Things* (1697/1951, p. 346), falls back on the Principle of Sufficient Reason in our making sense of whatever happens. He argues,

> The reasons of the world then lie in something extra-mundane, different from the chain of states, or series of things, whose aggregate constitutes the world. And so we must pass from the physical or hypothetical necessity, which determines the subsequent things of the world by the earlier, to something which is of absolute or metaphysical necessity, for which itself no reason can be given.

Proof from final causality (or design)

Earlier in this chapter, reference was made to the scientist Johannes Kepler's claim (quoted in Lennox, 2009, p. 21) that

> the chief aim of all explanations of the world would be to discover that the *rational order* which has been imposed upon it by God, and which has been revealed to us in the language of mathematics (this author's italics).

Such a 'rational order' shows how movement is explained not solely by 'efficient causes' (as explained above) but also by the pursuit of a pre-ordained end. David, the mathematician on the allotment, demonstrated this practically by showing how the petals of the chrysanthemum developed from the seeds according to the mathematical formulae of 'fibunaci'. The 'end purpose' of the flower's growth was potentially already present in its very beginning, becoming actual not randomly but according to built-in principles. And indeed the natural order reveals how different objects and species interconnect and are reconciled, again not randomly, but as though by design. As Etienne Gilson (1961, p. 75), in his exposition of Aquinas in the latter's *Summa Contra Gentiles*, explains,

> It is impossible that contrary and disparate things should be in accord and reconciled, either always or very often, unless there exists a being governing them and causing them collectively and individually to tend towards one determined end within the same order ... there must then exist a being by whose providence the world is governed, and it is this being that we call God.

The rational order, reflecting an overall 'design' as things move in harmony according to pre-ordained patterns of development, suggests a determining 'intelligence' – a cosmic mind, external to that material world, which provides an overall sense of purpose, a teleology, as different things move towards their own distinctive ends, albeit with reference to other evolving objects and species.

Such a brief entry into a long history of philosophical argument, beginning with Aristotle but continuing in much detailed nuancing to the present (witness Gilson, already referred to, or Teilhard De Chardin's teleological account of the universe in *The Phenomenon of Man*, 1959) may not provide 'proofs' in the strict sense as those referred to above, but it points to what many have seen as the 'reasonableness' of believing in a Being, external to and unlike the finite creatures in the material world (the 'Logos' of the opening words of St. John's Gospel), who provides the intelligent design as witnessed in the finite world.

In his 2003 book, *The Cosmic Habitat*, Martin Rees, Astronomer Royal and former president of the Royal Society wrote:

> The pre-eminent mystery is why anything should exist at all. What breathes life into the equations of physics, and actualises them in a real cosmos? Such questions lie beyond science, however: they are the province of philosophers and theologians.
>
> (p. 164)

Objectivity and evidence-based belief

Given the fallibility of human judgement ('Were my senses deceiving me?'; 'Was that the most acceptable way of verifying the conclusion reached?'; 'Is there a more appropriate way of viewing the data?'), and given also the often competing accounts of knowledge and of justifying belief, as described above, then whatever conclusions are reached frequently need to be tentative, subject to further examination and refined through the elimination of rival arguments and conclusions. 'Objectivity' lies in so presenting the tentative conclusions, such as those given above, that one would know what would cast doubt on the conclusions reached or what rival explanation should be preferred. 'Knowledge grows through criticism' as Popper (1972) argued. In light of that, one seeks evidence for conclusions rather than proof, always open to correction, new evidence and alternative interpretations.

Hence, the major religious traditions have themselves been developed over the millennia as a result of such scholarship, philosophical critique, theological argument and historical continuity. Within the Christian tradition (itself taking on board the profound philosophical labours of the ancient Greek civilisation), there is such critical and historical development combined with continuity within that tradition, as reflected in the constantly referenced contributions of Boethius' *Consolations of Philosophy* in the 5th century; of St. Augustine's struggles with Manicheism in the 4th century and of his introduction into theological discourse of Neoplatonism; of St. Thomas Aquinas' adoption of Aristotelian analysis to explore theological claims; and of the Islamic philosophers Avicenna and Averroes' development of Aristotelian philosophy, thereby contributing to the scholastic tradition of Western Europe. Thus, one might continue in the exposition of continuity, development and intellectual interchange between religious and non-religious traditions at the most profound level. Objectivity lies in this constant and developing critique of interacting traditions.

But does such a profound tradition, integrating in its development both Christian and Islamic philosophical thinking, produce 'certainty' – that state of mind which excludes doubt about the truth of a statement or beliefs and which seemed (come the Enlightenment) to be the product of the scientific revolution? And does such a tradition justify what Newman (1855) referred to as 'real assent'?

'Certainty' can arise from all sorts of evidence – for example, from the authority of trusted experts (as in accepting the conclusions of scientific reports on climate change), from logical argument (as in mathematics), from the result of a thorough appraisal of opposing views and the evidence for them and from direct observation. Although, in many claims to the truth, such certainty would logically (though not psychologically) seem to be unattainable, that should not detract necessarily from the reasonableness of conclusions reached, as in the case of religious knowledge and understanding (as illustrated in Chapter 2), or which, as explained above, from a long and developing critical tradition. Furthermore, where no one proposition *entails* a particular conclusion (for example, the existence of God), a collection of different sorts of propositions or strands of argument, pointing to the same conclusion, strongly suggest substantial support. But, as will be explained in Chapter 7, there are degrees of 'certainty' (and uncertainty) which, as recognised in the penultimate chapter, must be one of the 'challenges' for the teaching of religious education.

If such considerations were to be seen as inadequate reasons for teaching the truth of religious understanding within the educational environment, that same argument could equally be applied to other so-called forms of knowledge. Historical accounts, for example, cannot by their very nature be directly verified – one cannot go back in time. Historical judgments are made in the light of the best evidence available. New evidence is always being discovered and new interpretations given of what was previously believed, thereby requiring changes in the prevailing historical accounts.

So, too, is it with religious knowledge, which is based partly on historical scholarship, partly on consistent philosophical critique of claims being made, partly on making sense of the phenomenological experiences of holiness as described by such thinkers as Otto (see Chapter 2) and partly on what were referred to as 'proofs' by Aquinas (following Aristotle). In addition, reference has been made to the different ways in which people have come to believe in God – the 'mysterium tremendum'. And such overall 'reasonableness' (bringing all of these different kinds of evidence together) is re-enforced through the experience and language of rituals, but also (so it is claimed) through 'revelations', as will be explained in the following chapter.

Interim conclusion – giving assent

This introduction to knowledge, verification and evidence is intended as a preliminary comment on what can be reasonably thought about, come rationally to believe in and give one's assent to regarding the existence of God and indeed the nature of God. Already we have seen in Chapter 2 the development of belief in God which would not meet the criteria of knowledge as related to the logical requirements of Ayer's 'principle of verification'. But, in that respect, such reasoned beliefs share the same tentativeness as most claims to the truth. Therefore, it would be an exaggeration to accuse people of indoctrination simply because they had firm beliefs (for example, in holding certain moral principles) which did not measure up to the requirements of scientific verification. Indeed, the atheist, too, would fall into the category of 'the indoctrinated' for it is as difficult to prove the non-existence of God as it is to prove His existence. As Pascal proposes in *Pensees* (1670, p. 418) regarding 'the wager',

> though rational proof cannot establish the existence of God, nor can it establish God's non-existence – hence against reason to withhold judgment on this – the most important question in our lives. And you have no choice but to wager and/or to seek.

In what sense, therefore, can we, amongst so many rival claims and rival bases for claims, justify the *reasonableness* of believing in the existence of God and thereby in a commitment to a 'faith', as described in Chapter 2?

In *The Grammar of Assent*, John Henry Newman distinguished between 'notional assent' and 'real assent'. 'Notional assent' lies in following the reasoning within an argument to the conclusion which seems to follow but without that conclusion necessarily having any personal impact. Our general understanding of things in a personal or active sense remains much the same, as indeed in so much school-learning for examinations. 'Real assent', on the other hand, transforms one's personal experience of life; it has internalised that conclusion such that one thinks and feels differently about life, as when (according to Newman, 1855, p. 18) 'the works of St. Augustine bear witness to the spiritual history of their author'). The belief is more than a 'notional assent'. And this would illustrate the difference between a theological argument reaching a specific conclusion (as might be given in an academic seminar) and the absorption of the conclusion so as to come to live life in a different way. The conclusion – that *living faith* – may have been helped by the 'notional assents' arising from theological disputation, but it is something more than such an assent. Indeed, the theological disputation may well be but one element leading to the real assent, though accompanied, say, by the reading of the sayings of a holy person (see, for example, the transformation of Maggie in reading *Thomas a Kempis* in George Eliot's, 1872, *Mill on the* Floss, vol. 2, p. 32), or by observing the transformation of life within a religious community or by the aesthetic feelings arising from hearing beautifully sung Evensong. As indicated much earlier, real assent to a faith – to a religious form of living – arises not necessarily (or most likely) from any one source but from several sources, merging together as a powerful reason for committing oneself to a religious form of life.

Such 'real assent' would require something more than the 'notional assent' to there being an Infinite Being – the efficient and the final Cause, the First Mover and the Intelligent Designer, as arrived at through the 'proofs' as outlined above, but as such hardly describable in language, the meaning of which is located in the sensible world of finite things. Does not the 'real assent', as described above, require a more vivid picture of this Infinite Being, a connection between human modes of understanding and an understanding of the Divine? Can the reasonableness of belief in there being a God be extended to knowing something about the nature of that God to which one might give 'real assent'?

To that we must turn to the following chapter.

Bibliography

Aquinas, T., 1270 (circa), *Summa Theologica*.
Aquinas, T., 1265 (circa), *Summa Contra Gentiles*.
Aristotle, *Metaphysics*, see Everyman's Library (edited, 1956).
Augustus, St., 395, *Confessions*, Book VII, London: Fontana.
Ayer, A.J., 1936, *Language Truth and Logic*, London: Penguin.
Boethius, 5th Century, *De Consolatione Philosophiae*.
Brentano, F., 1874, *Psychology from the Empirical Standpoint*, London: Routledge edition.
Briggs, A., Steane, A., and Halvorson, H., 2018, *It Keeps Me Seeking*, Oxford: Oxford University Press.
Cooling, T., 1994, *A Christian Vision for State Education*, London: SPCQ.
Dawkins, R., 2006, *The God Delusion*, London: Bantam Press.
Dawkins, R., 2011, *New Statesman*, 19 December.
Eliot, G., 1878, *Mill on the Floss*, vol. 2, London: William Blackwood.

Gearon', L., 2014, *On Holy Ground: The Theory and Practice of Religious Education*, London: Routledge.
Gilson, E., 1961, *The Christian Philosophy of St. Thomas Aquinas*, London: Victor Gollancz, Ltd.
Gurney, P., 1981, *Behaviour Modification in Education*, University of Exeter.
Harlen, W., 2010, ed., *Principles and Big Ideas of Science Education*, Hatfield, Herts: Association of Science Education.
Harris, S., 2004, *The End of Faith: Religion, Terror, and the Future of Reason*, New York: W.W. Norton.
Heidegger, M., 1927, *Being and Time*, in F. Copleston, *History of Philosophy Vol. VII*, 1966, London: Burns and Oates.
Hitchins, C., 2007, *God Is Not Great*, Hatchet Book Group.
Hubery, D.S., 1972, *Christian Education in State and Church*, London: Denholm House Press.
Hume, D. 1751, *Enquiries Concerning the Human Understanding*, edited by L.A. Selby-Bigge.
Husserl, E., 1927, 'Phenomenology', *Journal of British Society for Phenomenology*, 2 (2).
James, W., 1902, *Varieties of Religious Experience*, London: Gifford Lectures.
Kant, I., 1784, *What Is Enlightenment?*
Kant, I., 1787, *Critique of Pure Reason*.
Kenny, A., (1992) *What Is Faith?* Oxford: Oxford University Press.
Leibniz, G.W., 1697, *On the Ultimate Origin of Things*, Leibniz Selections, 1951, New York: Scribner and Sons.
Lennox, J., 2009, *God's Undertaker: Has Science Buried God?* Oxford: Lion Hudson.
Locke, J., 1693, *Third Letter on Toleration*.
Lyotard, J.-F., 1984, *The Postmodern Condition: A Report on Knowledge*, Minneapolis: University of Minnesota Press.
MacIntyre, A., 2009, *God, Philosophy, Universities*, London: Continuum.
Newman, J.H., 1855, *Grammar of Assent*, New York: Image Books, 1955 edition.
Otto, R., 1923/1958, *The Idea of the Holy*, Oxford: Oxford University Press.
Pascal, E., 1670, *Pensees*, ed. Krailsheimer, A.J., Harmondsworth: Penguin.
Popper, K., 1972, *Objective Knowledge: An Evolutionary Approach*, Oxford: Clarendon Press.
Popper, K., 2002, *Conjectures and Refutations: The Growth of Scientific Knowledge*, London: Routledge.
Rees, M., 2003, *The Cosmic Habitat*, London: Phoenix.
Sharpe, E.F., 1975, 'The phenomenology of religion', in *Learning for Living*, 15(1).
Smart, N., 1968, *Secular Education and the Logic of Religion*, London: Faber and Faber.
Stern, J., 2018, *A Celebration of Truth and Uncertainty in Both Religious Education and Science*, Unpublished Paper, York St. John University.
Swinburne, R., 2004, *The Existence of God*, 3rd ed., Oxford: Clarendon Press.
Teilhard de Chardin, P., 1959, *The Phenomenon of Man*, London: William Collins.
Thomas a Kempis, T., 1425/1952, *Of the Imitation of Christ*, London: Burns an Oates.
Wilkinson, J.A., 2015, *A Fresh Look at Islam in a Multi-faith World*, London: Routledge.
Wittgenstein, L., 1958, *Philosophical Investigations*, Oxford: Basil Blackwell.
Wright, A., 2007, *Critical Religious Education, Multiculturalism and the Pursuit of Truth*, Cardiff University Press, pp. 196–200.
Young, M.F.D., ed., 1972, *Knowledge and Control*, London: Methuen.

4

UNDERSTANDING THE NATURE OF GOD

Difficulties are necessarily encountered (even where belief in God's existence and 'having a faith' are accepted) (as described in Chapters 2 and 3), if we are to relate to God and to live a distinctively religious life, since it would be necessary to know not only that God exists but also 'as what' he exists. Was Aquinas correct in saying that we can know rationally that there is a God but not what God is? Does such knowledge (essential for a religious form of life and religious formation) depend therefore not on reason alone but also on revelation – a further concept which requires explanation?

Introduction

Chapter 2 referred to the paradox in the statement of Aquinas, namely, that knowledge of God consists in knowing *that* He is but not knowing *what* He is. Was Aquinas but repeating the sentiments of St. Augustine in his *Sermons*, namely, *Si comprehendis, non est Deus* ('if you understand, it is not God')? Or of the 8th-century John of Damascus, impeccably orthodox, who wrote:

> It is plain, then, that there is a God. But what he is in his essence and nature is absolutely incomprehensible and unknowable.
> *(quoted in Harries, 2002, p. 145)*

But religion and a religious life surely require awareness, not just of the 'mysterium tremendum', referred to in Chapter 2, but also something of its nature, howsoever mysterious. How can one worship that about which one knows nothing? And that, as pointed out by Keith Ward (2015, p. 1) in his 'little book of guidance' entitled, *What do we mean by God?*, is not made easier by some of the images of God in great works of art such as that by Michelangelo on the ceiling of the Sistine Chapel in Rome, where God is shown

> as a very well-developed, well-muscled specimen of humanity with long white hair and a flowing beard.

There are four answers to this puzzle which need to be considered:

(i) understandings which arise from attempts to 'prove' the existence of God;
(ii) identification of characteristics of God's nature by analogy with our understanding of human nature;
(iii) revelation, through God's self – disclosure, manifest in the testimony of Moses and the prophets as reported in the Old Testament, or in the life of Jesus Christ as reported in the New Testament, or in the revelations to Mohammad in the Qur'an;
(iv) participation in a spiritual tradition.

(i) Understanding through attempts to 'prove' God's existence

The word 'prove' is placed in inverted commas because it is necessary to distinguish (as explained in Chapter 3) proof in this religious context from the logical certainty, which is characteristic of mathematical proof or pure logic. Rather it is used in the sense in which one speaks of 'strong evidence' being the basis of a belief, as in the case of most everyday practical conclusions. For example, there is no 'proof', strictly speaking, that it will rain tomorrow, but the evidence would indicate strongly that it will. Nonetheless, influential attempts have been made to expound such 'proofs' (as illustrated in the last chapter, following the lead of Aristotle, and much discussed ever since – see Gilson, 1961, Chapter 5, 'The Attributes of God'). They may not provide the *conclusive* 'proof', which that word now demands, but that should not deflect from the power of the arguments which they convey, moving from the finite and physical world to a more comprehensive explanation of that world (the '*meta-physical*'). The fact that we cannot have *knowledge* of God, as argued by Kant (1785), does not entail the impossibility of a reality beyond the world of phenomena which in some sense makes that world intelligible and which in various ways enters into very different modes of seeing, appreciating and relating to it. Lack of *knowledge* does not entail the unreasonableness of *belief*. Indeed, as Kant stated, in *The Critique of Pure Reason* (1781), 'I have therefore found it necessary to deny knowledge in order to make room for faith'.

On the other hand, in seeing the material world as the 'effect' of a Divine Being, that 'effect' need not tell us anything about *the nature* of what was referred to as the 'Cause', and which (let us remember from Chapter 2 above) is the 'mysterium tremendum', who *transcends* understanding. In describing the finite effect, can we relate such description to the nature of the ultimate Cause? Indeed, even within the finite or created world, 'effects' do not necessarily share the characteristics of that which has caused them, as when the ball moves when it is kicked – although, of course, there are examples of where there are such relationships between cause and effect, as when the seeds of an older plant are used to propagate a new plant. But the 'proof' for the existence of God from the effects of 'efficient causality' would not necessarily show in those effects the characteristic of the Divine Being who caused those effects.

But perhaps progress can be made. The 'proof' pointing to God as the 'Final Cause', responsible for the overall *design and sense of purpose* of the teleological world as we know it, suggests strongly an 'intelligence', as that might be understood within the world of finite human beings, though inadequately when applied to God. Modern science abhors randomness and assumes that the universe can ultimately be understood within the system of physical laws either already discovered or to be discovered. But such an abhorrence of randomness would seem applicable to 'the system as a whole', and thus implicitly show the signs of intelligent design. However, this can lead only to partial understanding – that is, understanding, one might say, by analogy. Such a God would be both like and unlike the intelligent beings (the 'designers') we are familiar with. Hence, we need to look further at the idea, analogously speaking, by which we might transfer to God the human notion of intelligence (and indeed other qualities within human nature).

(ii) Understanding through analogy

Therefore, traditional attempts to prove God's existence (as reflected in Chapter 3) should not be confused with the logical certainty of mathematical proofs, but, given their validity, they indicate attributes which are comprehensible within ordinary human communication, as when we attribute to God 'knowledge' (as in the case of 'omniscience') or 'power' (as in 'omnipotence') or 'intelligence' (as explained above) or in being a 'person'. On the other hand, can descriptions attributed to finite creatures (such as 'knowing' or 'power' or 'intelligence' or 'personal'), which arise from everyday sensible experience, be transferred to God, who is not open to such experience and whose existence has been made aware of through a different mode of reasoning, as reflected in Chapters 2 and 3? Is it a case of God's attributes being recognised at one level but (as asserted by Isaiah) 'enclosed in majesty, mystery and awfulness'?

Here it is important to distinguish between the univocal, equivocal, and analogous application or use of concepts.

One would be using a concept *univocally* where it has exactly the same meaning in its description of very different objects or situations, as when one calls both a cat and a board black. That clearly is not the case where, for instance, we attribute 'caring' or 'forgiving' to both God and human beings. There is sufficient likeness between the different applications for the use in the human context to enable us to have some insight into its application to the divine context. But the contexts are so different that our use of such concepts in the finite world can but give an intimation of its significance in the divine life.

On the other hand, a term is used *equivocally* where the concept or term is used in an ambiguous sense, when there may be, for instance, an historical or other link in its two usages. It may well be the case, for example, that, over time and resulting from social pressure and changes, the concept of 'university' as a place of higher learning through scholarship, research and teaching, has arguably come to mean something very different (although trading upon the *emotive* use of the term in its original meaning) through the privatization and changed purposes of such so-called institutions – for example, in the case of 'business schools' or the now defunct Trump University (see Pring, 2018, ch. 8, When is a University not a university?).

Therefore, those who claim agnosticism in our knowledge and understanding of God might well accuse the theist of *equivocation* (that is, of misusing concepts either by likening God to what we understand of human beings), or of *univocal* misuse – that is, by arguing that this is a total misuse of words, taking them from one context (that of human beings) and applying the apparently *same words* to an entirely different context, although (in the case of 'equivocation') with certain common features which (unlike in the case of the 'black cat' and the 'black board') make the identification somewhat plausible.

Therefore, in being conscious of the *intelligibility* of the universe (the natural laws through which we come to understand how things work and how we can predict what will happen), one might well ascribe intelligence to the 'designing' of that universe. But, whilst understanding what that means from our normal usage of the term, we have to recognise that such intelligence, when applied outside the finite world in which we have come to use it, is remarkably more comprehensive and powerful than what finite human beings can grasp or imagine. Thus we might say that the word is used *analogously*, giving insight into God's nature, albeit imperfectly – as when, in the Muslim *basmala*, children are taught to say 'in the name of God, the merciful, the compassionate'.

However, intelligence is but one significant aspect of something being a 'person'. In that respect, whom we see as a person is an object with which it is possible to engage personally (in the religious context, through prayer or through seeking God's will for us). Again we are employing a concept 'person' which is central to our lives within the finite world which we inhabit, but which becomes a crucial aspect in our making sense of that God in whom we have come to believe, albeit once again in a magnified and analogous sense.

Furthermore, when we reflect on what makes us distinctively human persons, we cannot ignore in particular the pursuit of a moral life defined by the virtues (more of which in Chapter 5), and so by analogy we might see such virtues to be characteristic, albeit in a magnified degree, of the Being in whom perfection is to be found – reflected in the hopeful plea to 'our Father' to 'forgive us our trespasses as we forgive those who trespass against us'. And every chapter of the Qur'an, except one, begins with the phrase, 'In the name of God, the Universally Merciful, the Intensely Merciful'.

By analogy with our human understanding and exercise of mercy, we might (with reasonable hope) attribute such a quality of mercy to the ultimate goal of our moral life, the pursuit of which has too often been imperfect. And, of course, when Jesus spoke of God as the Father, the word 'father' was not used in exactly the same sense as we normally use it but was drawing attention *analogously*, based on human experience and reality, to a mode of relating to the person of God as revealed.

A 'by-product' of the resort to analogy in order to grasp, however inadequately, the attributes of God, is what Aquinas, in his *Summa Theologica* (Ia), referred to as the 'via negativa', asserting what God is not! Another way of putting it, according to Austin Farrer (and once again quoted by Harries, 2002, p. 146)

> every image of God must be broken and then remade, and then broken again endlessly.

(iii) Understanding through revelation

There are many things which we come to know about other people, not through observation of them or their actions, but through *self-disclosure* of their feelings, motives and aspirations. Given there is a God, it is perfectly possible that God should disclose to humanity more than the abstractions referred to above. It is the belief of the three Abrahamic faiths that this is what God did through Jesus Christ, Muhammad, Moses and the prophets. God (unknowable in His essence by reason alone) revealed Himself in human form, as expressed in the Old and New Testaments or in the Qur'an.

Such revelation, therefore, is not to individuals isolated from communities, but rather from such unfolding traditions. There are histories of spiritual insights arising from such 'divine self-disclosures', as given in the Old and New Testaments and in the Qur'an. Such enduring spiritual insights, the holy lives that are inspired by them, and the philosophical reflections upon such insights and upon such lives offer some understanding of what God might be 'as a person' and thereby open to a relationship through contemplation and through prayer – a matter of a tentative 'faith seeking understanding' (*fides quaerens intellectum* in the words of St. Anselm). Thus, what Christians believe to be the self-disclosure of God in human (and thereby accessible) form through the *incarnation* of Jesus Christ would also be understood as a key element in the stories of revelation as given through the prophets in the Old Testament. Indeed, it would be seen as a participation in the old Hebrew tradition of attempting

> to rationalize, moralise and humanise the idea of God – a living factor in the Prophets and in the psalms, continuously bringing the apprehension of the numinous to a richer fulfilment by recognizing in it attributes of clear and profound value for the reason.
>
> *(source of quote unknown)*

Inevitably the question must be raised about the validity of any claim to divine self-disclosure. Many have been the false prophets through history to invent such claims.

But some retain a highly plausible and compelling influence, generate a profound spiritual tradition, survive examination of even the least likely claims (for example, the Resurrection) and generate a long tradition of critical scholarship.

Furthermore, the forms of life which such claims generate give credibility to the validity of the claimed revelation. This is clearly the case with the foundations of Christianity, as reflected in the accounts given in the Gospels, in the Letters of the Apostles to the early Christians rapidly scattered around the Middle East, and to the quick growth of systematic philosophical reflections upon the early revelations, as in the works of Boethius or of St. Augustine. But, similarly, the continuity with and growth from the Prophets of the Old Testament reflect powerfully this gradual self-disclosure of the otherwise 'Deus Absconditus'.

One might speak similarly of the beginning, spread and spiritual influence of the Islamic tradition revealed to Mohammed on Mount Hira, developed in the writings of the Qur'an and inspiring a world-wide spiritual tradition and way of life.

(iv) Understanding through participation in a spiritual tradition

Nonetheless, as Austin Farrer (1957, p. 91) points out,

> It is not I to whom God is revealed, it is the people of God in all their persons, time and places, and if I will not look with them I need not hope to see.

As Farrer continues his account of revelation, he points to the value of the historical development – the increased enlightenment – through reflection within a spiritual tradition. The beginnings of such a spiritual tradition will doubtless be captured in the stories and accounts of key books within that tradition – for example, the 'Parable of the Prodigal Son' or of the 'Rich Man and Lazarus' in St. Luke's Gospel (ch.15), the stories of Jewish hope and destiny through persecution and travail, or the accounts of the developing Islamic self-knowledge and forms of life as given in the Qur'an and the Hadith. The significance and practical influence of such stories become more central through the regular re-telling, further commentary and practical implementation.

Traditions evolve through practical and critical engagement within a community. Other persons' enlightenment (mystics, generally acknowledged holy people, philosophers and theologians) contributes to such and becomes the basis of further growth in understanding within that wider community. The insights of St. Paul build on the prophecies of Isaiah and illuminate the understandings and the forms of life of the early Christian communities – and, thereafter, are open to further insight through the practices, worship, liturgy and meditations of the evolving Church, but also through the sifting out of 'false prophecies'.

There are similarities here with how the 'Sharia' (which is Arabic for 'pathway') relates the actions concerned with daily life (for example, the giving of alms) with actions concerned with relationship with God (for example, the daily responses to the call to prayer), whereby

> constraining the outer human person to some immanent obligation of behavior, liberates the inner self for engagement with transcendentally emancipatory meaning, [thus] the traditional spiritual structure of Islamic praxis – belief, outer obligatory worship, the derivation of inner spiritual meaning.
> (Wilkinson, 2015, p. 97)

There is something remarkable in the longevity, and yet evolution through constant critique, of the great spiritual traditions – ones which generate yet further insights through the lives and writings of recognised holy people such as (for example, within Christianity) St. Francis of Assisi or St. Teresa of Avila, both of whom instituted religious orders which, with their distinctive interpretations of the religious form of life, continue to give insight into the spiritual life.

Interim conclusion

The ultimate purpose of this book is to reflect upon the nature of religious education in our schools, with particular reference to the reasonableness (and thus the truth) of religious beliefs. At the very first (as in Chapter I), this was commenced through a critical look at the evolution of religious education as schools come to reflect the more secular nature of society (wherein the rational basis for religious belief is increasingly doubted, as will be argued further in Chapter 8). Secondly, therefore, the chapters which followed attempted to show by contrast that there is such a basis on which religious understanding and formation might be promoted, both through the 'reasonableness' of believing in God (even if that does not amount to 'knowledge', as that word has come to be meant – see Chapter 3), and through the systematic critiques of the nature of God, as that has been relayed in this chapter.

These purposes, however, need to address, in Chapter 9, 'the challenge' to religious education arising from the diversity and the absence of religious beliefs amongst those being educated. Religious education inevitably means something different where that is pursued in a very secular context, as opposed to one where pupils have already been initiated to some degree into religious beliefs and practices. But even in this latter case, the range of difference in faith and practice is such that to see how religious 'reasonableness' and then formation might in general be promoted is not easy. To this problem we shall return in Chapter 8.

However, the argument so far has been that, given religious belief to be 'reasonable', as argued in the earlier chapters (even if open to doubt – see Chapter 7), then it is necessary to examine the ways in which such belief is open to greater understanding. That required addressing the different sorts of account by which we might enter into the mysteries of the divine – not just that God exists but also the nature of that God. In so doing, the account so far has drawn upon the different religious and philosophical traditions through which the nature of God has been reflected upon, especially the Aristotelian understanding, adopted by the Scholastic and Islamic philosophers, which *inter alia* argued for an 'intelligent designer' as an explanation of such a mathematically organised and intelligible universe.

Perhaps the position we have reached is best summed up by Keith Ward (2015, p. 23), thus:

> This argument for God, therefore, points us in a certain direction – in the direction of greater and greater understanding. But it points to something beyond our experience, an idea which we cannot really grasp. And this is just where the argument becomes more than merely abstract (like some purely academic exercise), because it is in fact an exercise in the training of a vision, in pointing our minds towards a reality just 'beyond' our understanding, but in the direction of greater, not less, understanding.

One way in which the argument becomes more than 'merely abstract', but which so far has been hardly touched upon, is through examination of the *moral dimension* of our lives and the urge to have some overall purpose which shapes what we value and to what we are committed. Such an overall purpose may seem relatively trivial to some – for example, to be an international football player, though to the person concerned it may outweigh all other conceptions of the good life to be pursued. But, given the pitfalls and disappointments on the way, and no doubt the need to change direction, there is the beginning of the examination of the 'life worth living'. Most of us will be called upon to tackle such a task at least once in our lives, according to Descartes (*First Meditation*, para.1). The task is given moral significance by Socrates: 'The unexamined life is not worth living for a human being' (Plato, 38a).

Such an examination, taken more seriously by some and possibly not taken seriously by others, takes us into considerations of the moral life – consideration of the life worth living, the values to be pursued, the virtues to be nurtured and the duties to be adopted. This we need to consider more systematically in the following chapter as one possible route to the divine.

Bibliography

Aquinas, T., *Summa Theologica*.
Augustine, St., 5th Century, *Sermons*.
Cottingham, J., 2009, *Why Believe?* London: Continuum.
Farrer, A., 1957, 'Revelation', in Mitchell, B., ed., *Faith and Logic*, London: George, Allen and Unwin, Ltd.
Gilson, E., 1961, *The Christian Philosophy of St. Thomas Aquinas*, London: Victor Gollancz.
Harries, R., 2002, *God Outside the Box*, London: SPCK.
Kant, I., 1781, *Critique of Pure Reason*.

Kant, I., 1785, *Groundwork, or Fundamental Principles, of the Metaphysics of Morals*, Plato, *Apology*.
Pring, R., 2018, 'When is a university not a university?' *Thinking Philosophically About Education*, London: Routledge.
Ward, K., 2015, *What Do We Mean By God?* London: SPCK.
Wilkinson, M., 2015, *A Fresh Look at Islam in a Multi-Faith World*, London: Routledge.

5

THE MORAL DIMENSION

Has God got a place within it?

The philosophical arguments continue with a consideration of the moral dimension of, and reasoning behind, a faith-based form of life (and thus initiation into such a life through schools' educational programmes). Such a consideration has two dimensions: first, the extent to which moral awareness, systematically reflected on, is a further indication of God's existence, thereby providing further evidence for believing and for a distinctively religious form of life. The second dimension (given God's existence and His nature, as revealed in different ways) concerns the need to ask whether specific moral consequences follow. For example, would the committed religious practitioner, if being consistent with his or her religious beliefs, be thinking morally and acting differently from the serious secular thinker and reformer?

On being human

An oft-quoted letter (see Strom, 1981, p. 4) sent by an American high school principal, who was a survivor of a concentration camp, to newly appointed teachers, declared,

> My request is: help your students become human. Your efforts must never produce learned monsters, skilled psychopaths, educated Eichmans. Reading, writing, and arithmetic are important but only if they serve to make our children more human.

What, then, is it to become 'more human'? What are those aspects of being human which, though potentially there at birth, need to be developed, especially through education, if we are to be *fully* human? Furthermore, is there a religious dimension to that 'becoming more human' of which the education of young people needs to take account?

Here, however, there is a difficulty. Might not people have their own ideas about what it means to be 'fully human' – a seemingly relative concept – and thus choose to develop in different directions, including those directions which have no religious dimension?

On the other hand, would it be possible, on the basis of reasoning, to show the *required* direction for that development to take place in order for such people to become *fully* human, even though each individual has the free will to choose not to be so? Is being 'fully human' a state of being which is not a subjective or personal choice but which meets standards and values which are rationally defensible?

There are three aspects of what it means to be, and therefore to develop as, a human being which are relevant to the educational argument.

The first concerns the development of knowledge and understanding – learning to participate in what Michael Oakeshott (1933) referred to as 'the conversation between the generations of mankind', namely, the different 'voices' of science, of history, of philosophy, of poetry, of religion and so on, through which one comes to understand both oneself and the physical and social worlds which one inhabits and therefore the values which are assumed in those different voices. Human development, therefore, would include this capacity to think intelligently (that is, to learn how to engage in that 'conversation') and, in so doing, to draw upon what others have said and written in shaping their futures and therefore in what is embedded in the inherited cultures as to what can be meant by 'becoming more human'.

A second aspect of being human lies in recognising the social dimension of one's life – the interactions with other people in the community through providing and receiving mutual support and co-operation, through creating the social and civil frameworks for that to happen and through thinking about the future which necessarily has to be shared in harmony with others. Out of such shared thinking arise such procedural values as justice and fairness through which differences might be reconciled.

But, thirdly, and most importantly for our purposes, 'becoming more human' requires gaining the ability to engage practically with the demands of life – in particular the practical ability to make choices concerning what to do in particular situations and thereby (underlying such particular choices) to reflect implicitly on the sort of life which one wants to lead and which is embodied in those choices. Such reflection on the best way forward would imply some consideration of the sort of human being one wants to become in the light of the understandings which have been gained through experience, through the 'conversation between the generations', through the different influences which have impinged on one's life and through the interrelationships with others within one's society – contemplating alternative ways of living and shaping one's life accordingly. Each person has within him or herself, from conception, the pre-ordained growth to become the being which he or she does become, although affected in that growth by interaction with other people and thoughts about what is worthwhile.

On the other hand, such a human being has the intelligence and freedom to affect that interaction – to determine the ends to which that continued growth will be directed. The end to be attained is not absolutely fixed. Indeed, the end which is to shape human development is partly of the person's choosing. Thereby the concept of 'final causality' enters into our understanding of moral life – namely, understanding oneself as goal directed, as one who is moved not only by one's physical nature, but also by one's choices from childhood onwards towards a conception (at least implicitly) of what seems to be a fulfilled life, a life of 'human flourishing'.

Implicit, therefore, in the cultural (including religious) inheritance which one has received, in the social and civil contexts in which one lives, and in the choices which one makes, are the underlying values which are thought worth pursuing, even if, initially, they are but implicit in one's daily living. Part of growing up must be to make those values more explicit and to be open to questions as to whether they do constitute a worthwhile form of life. In this way one is drawn into ethics, namely, reasoning about the sort of life worth living, from which religious considerations cannot be excluded.

However, there would seem to be no simple answers to such questions, as is obvious from the struggles and disagreements amongst philosophers from Aristotle onwards. Indeed, as pointed out in Chapter 3, some philosophers would argue that there can be no rational way forward in determining whether one form of life is objectively better than another. According to David Hume (1751) in his *Inquiry Concerning the Principle of Morals*, conclusions drawn from any basis other than purely logical premises, or from what can be sensibly observed (as in science), should be 'committed to the flames for it can contain nothing but sophistry' (XII, Part III). Therefore, there is no objective or rational way, so it is argued, for deciding that one form of life is better than another. As explained in Chapter 3, with reference to Professor Ayer's (1936) 'emotive theory of ethics', human flourishing or the values thought worth pursuing are seen to be but a matter of personal and subjective choice. 'Self-expression' and self-fulfilment', without reference to external standards as to what is worthwhile, become a dominant aim. Richard Harries (2002, p. 130) thus quotes Herman Hesse, the German novelist:

> When a man tries, with the gifts bestoweed upon him by nature, to fulfil himself he is doing the highest thing he can do, the only thing that has any meaning.

The examined life: duty and conscience

By contrast with the above objection to addressing rationally the values to be pursued in life, it was the claim of Socrates at his trial before the court at Athens, and answering the charge that he 'had corrupted the minds of the young', that the 'unexamined life is not worth living' (Plato *Apology*). Getting the youth of Athens to examine their lives had been part of Socrates' mission. But the 'examined life' requires the giving of reasons as to what is or is not worth living for. Therefore, it is to the distinctive type of reasoning in addressing the 'examined life' to which we must turn, starting with what, in the words of the American principal, 'makes our children more human'.

The first aspect of what constitutes 'more human' concerns the manner in which one lives and relates to other people – the 'dispositions' through which one sees people or problems in a particular way and relates to them accordingly. Such dispositions or virtues (those, for example, of caring, compassion, patience, courage) have their contrary dispositions or vices (those of indifference, lack of sympathy, impatience, cowardice), and therefore the virtues are in need of nurturing so that one learns how to be virtuous and thereby how to see, and thus act towards, situations and people in a humane way. Learning to be 'fully human' would seem to require the development of such dispositions and virtues, often demanding a struggle against the temptations to pursue a self-centred and pleasure-seeking life.

The second, though connected, aspect of such an 'examined life' lies in the sense of duty, the 'having a conscience' about matters for which one can, and should, be held responsible and about the manner of conducting oneself as is reflected in the different virtues. Such conscience is shown in the use of the word 'ought'. 'Ought' is used in two different, but related, senses. When one says, 'If you want to get to London by 10 a.m., you *ought* to catch that bus', one is using the word purely hypothetically – 'catching the bus' is a necessary means to achieving a specific goal, whether or not such a goal is worth pursuing. However, when one uses the word 'ought' categorically, as when one says, 'You *ought not* to tell a lie', then one is proclaiming an absolute value, one which is held neither as a means to some further end nor as a personal choice.

The question then concerns how far would it be possible to live with others in society, first, in a totally non-virtuous way (for even amongst thieves there must be a sense of loyalty) and, second, without any sense of duty – without submitting to an 'unconditional ought'?

That would be extremely difficult because of the obligations which arise from the inevitable social relations with others in the community, as in the case, for example, of making promises. 'To promise' would not make sense unless it carried an obligation to do as one said one would, and that must logically be recognised even when one does not intend to carry out the promise – when, for instance, one is telling a lie.

However, more needs to be said about the nature and relation of *reasoning* to the recognition of such obligations, to how such obligations may be put into practice, and especially to those obligations which form one's conscience. Such a case needs to be made, given the objections raised by Hume, namely, that the connections between 'what is the case' and 'what ought to be the case' is 'nothing but sophistry' (see quote above) – or indeed raised by Ayer in his 'emotive theory of ethics, also referred to above.

The philosopher Immanuel Kant, 1783, in *Prolegomena to Any Future Metaphysics*, declared that it was David Hume who first interrupted his dogmatic slumbers. Therefore, in the conclusion of *Critique of Practical Reason*, 1788, he wrote of the strange compelling power of the moral values which call forth our allegiance – far from being 'nothing but sophistry' of which Hume had written. The purpose of, and the requirement for, *practical* reasoning is the prescription to action, which prescription could be either very specific (you should get up at 6 a.m.) or open to several possibilities (you should get up early). However, as stated above, it is important to distinguish in such practical reasoning between hypothetical prescription (you should get up early if you want to go swimming) and the categorical prescription (you should get up early – no ifs, ands or buts). But then you could ask on what grounds does one have to accept such a categorical prescription, and the answer would lie in an even more general prescription – until one is finally appealing to a fundamental and universalisable principle which one would wish to be seen as a universal practical rule appropriate for all human beings.

That is expressed by Kant (1785), with characteristic lack of clarity, in *The Groundwork of the Metaphysics of Morals*:

> I am never to act otherwise than so that I can also will that my maxim should become a universal law.

By 'maxim' is meant the grounds or principles on which one makes a decision to act in a particular way. But such a decision is always open to questioning, and therefore one needs to go more deeply and to justify it in terms of a more comprehensive principle until at last one reaches the ultimate principle – that which is seen to be universalisable to everyone in similar situations. One element in such a universal principle, which permeates all of our obligations, is the treatment of other people as 'ends in themselves' that is, not merely as the means to something one wants. Thus, in *The Groundwork,* Kant expresses this as follows:

> So act as to treat humanity, whether in your own person or in that of any other, always at the same time as an end, and never merely as a means.

This notion of the universalisation of principles must give the force to all moral reasoning; it is the general rule to which one appeals and which one would wish to be true of everyone, thereby creating the sense of duty to a way of life of universal application. And, in so acting, one is asserting and showing the autonomy which becomes the rational person. Persons, in working out their ultimate goals or way of life (in terms, for example, of living a virtuous life), and in pursuing them whatever the difficulties faced, are acting as truly rational agents and thus as ends in themselves, not determined primarily by personal desires, interests or passing fads.

'Duty' therefore embodies the requirement that anyone in a similar position would be seen to reach the same conclusion as to what one ought to do. Such moral reasoning is, according to Kant, quite distinctive from the hypothetical reasoning where one is simply pointing to the necessary or likely means for achieving a specific goal, which itself need not carry any specific obligation. The duty to tell the truth or not to kill other human beings depends not on empirical experience (*a posteriori* conditions of one's particular situation) but on what it means to engage in practical reasoning about how to live (the *a priori* condition of so reasoning).

Inevitably there often comes a clash between the *a priori* requirements of such practical reasoning, as when, for example, 'telling a lie' might be necessary to 'saving a life'. But that simply requires seeking a more comprehensive principle which, say, prioritises 'saving a life' over 'telling the truth', bearing in mind the context in which the choice has to be made. There is no escape from the imperative of such moral deliberation, seeking to achieve the most universal principles and values to which different societies should conduct themselves, as is illustrated by the United Nations' *Convention on Civil and Political Rights* and *Convention on Social, Cultural and Economic Rights*.

Therefore, Kant states at the beginning of *The Groundwork of the Metaphysics of Morals*,

> It is impossible to conceive of anything in the world, or indeed out of it, which can be called good without qualification save only a good will.

And 'good will' is that seeking (in any situation) to follow one's conscience as described above, irrespective of the material or other consequences and disappointments which might arise in so doing.

Do moral duty and conscience point to a supreme source of what is good?

That 'good will', bringing the 'categorical practical reason' to bear upon the choices on how best to live, is embedded in what we call 'conscience' – that 'inner voice' which nags away at one as one faces difficult decisions. At first, the formation of such a conscience – the bringing together of the several duties and the virtues (but also the personal interests and desires) by which one conducts one's life – can be a struggle. But eventually that 'coming together' shapes a coherent life in terms of how one should live – the 'good life'.

Such a conscience, which welcomes (despite the difficulties which it may entail) what is believed to be the way one ought to live, is seen by some to be yet a further sign of God within human consciousness. According to Kant (1797), God's existence cannot be proved because God lies outside the phenomenal world, the world of empirical experience. But that existence can be reasonably 'postulated' as an explanation of the moral force of conscience – a presupposition of practical rational thinking about how life should be lived. It therefore gives grounds for faith, if not for knowledge.

Similarly for Newman (1955, p. 98), though of course from within a deeply religious background,

> [conscience] is a moral sense, and a sense of duty; a judgement of the reason and a magisterial dictate . . . its testimony [is] that there is a right and a wrong, and its sanction to that testimony conveyed in the feelings which attend on right or wrong conduct.

The feelings accompanying the moral judgment (the 'moral sense') are those such as self-reproach, shame, and remorse, where one has transgressed the voice of conscience. But such strong feelings, such sense of transgression and such 'magisterial dictate' seem to imply an exterior authority and force.

Thus, elsewhere, Newman argues,

> Conscience is the essential principle and sanction of Religion in the mind. Conscience implies a relation between the soul and a something exterior, and that moreover superior, to itself; a relation to an excellence which it does not possess, and to a tribunal over which it has no power. And since the more closely this inner monitor is respected and followed, the clearer, the more exalted, and the more varied its dictates become, and the standard of excellence is ever outstripping (while it guides) our obedience, a moral conviction is thus at length obtained of the unapproachable nature as well as the supreme authority of *That*, whatever it is, which is the object of the mind's contemplation.
>
> (Newman, 1826/1843, quoted in MacIntyre, 2009, p. 141)

Therefore, do these demands of conscience – this sense of duty as to how life should be lived in terms of the virtues to be developed and in terms of the ends to be pursued, irrespective of personal temptations and desires – point to a Being, a presence, that sets the standards of what counts as being 'fully human'? Such was the conclusion of Kant's 'postulation' of such a being in order to make sense of the moral force of conscience. And such was Newman's conclusion in relation to an 'excellence which it does not possess' and to a 'tribunal over which it has no power'.

Such a consideration of the imperative nature of conscience does not add up to 'proof' as it has been described earlier (pp. 34–37), but it does provide reason for such a faith when combined with the other reasons as described in Chapter 3. It is a strand of thinking which, combined with other strands referred to, leads one in a particular direction – to faith in a God, which may not carry absolute certainty, but provides reasonable grounds for belief nonetheless.

It is relevant at this moment to be reminded of what a denial of such a conclusion might entail – namely, radical existential choice. Thus, Sartre (1959) wrote, quoting initially Dostoevski:

> If God did not exist, everything would be permitted, and that, for existentialism, is the starting point.

Do moral consequences follow from a religious form of life?

The second dimension of the relationship between morality and religion lies in the implications which a religious form of life has for the way we behave. Thus, given 'religious faith' for whatever reasons (and those reasons, not certainties, have been outlined above and more particularly in the previous chapters), is there not more to say about the relation of religious belief to the moral life? So far (the first dimension), one has moved from the moral life, as embodied in the conscience, to the *postulation* of God as the force behind that conscience. But now it is important to move in the opposite direction – from the belief in God to a distinctive way of life, which seems common to the Abrahamic religions (Judaism, Christianity and Islam). Such a move seems clear from the texts of those different religious beliefs.

With regard to Christianity, the overriding counsel of perfection might be summed up in the following claim by Jesus:

> A new commandment I give to you, that you love one another: as I have loved you, that you also love one another.
>
> *(John 13:14)*

And such a commandment was vigorously followed up on by St. Paul, as in his letter to the Corinthians (1:13):

> In a word, there are three things that last for ever: faith, hope and love, but the greatest of them all is love.

That 'loving one another' is reflected in the many prescriptions on how to relate to one another in terms of 'forgiveness for wrongs done', or of 'support for the poor and the sick' or of 'pursuit of peace'. Perhaps it is best summarised in the eleven Beatitudes given in the Gospels (see St. Matthew's Gospel, Chapter 5). But it enters into a view of society as reflected in Pope Leo XIII's influential Encyclical, *Rerum Novarum*, in 1875, in defining 'the common good' and thus the conception of the Early Church as reflected in the Acts of the Apostles (2:41–47):

> All whose faith had drawn them together held everything in common; they would sell their property and possessions and make a general distribution as the need of each required.

With regard to Islam, the Qur'an (81.26) offers guidance for all humanity:

> To show human beings the way to live in accordance with the will of God.

'Sadaqa' or 'bearing one another's burdens', follows the underlying principle of one's relation to all humanity, especially to those in need. These very general principles are spelt out in many specific exhortations and are embodied in ways of living. The Five Pillars of Islam, as revealed in the Qur'an, provide that daily awareness of God and of one's way of living within the spirit of Islam, namely, professing and practising the principal beliefs of Islam, ritual prayer five times a day, giving of one's wealth to the poor ('zakat'), fasting during the month of Ramadan and making the pilgrimage ('Hajj') to Mecca at least once in a lifetime. Within Islam ('Islam' meaning the state of perfect harmony between God and all creation), through the books of guidance (the Qur'an and the 'Sunna', meaning a pattern of behaviour that the people should follow), we have been called to live an ethical life following the revealed will of God. Hence, the key importance of the 'Shari'a', namely 'a pathway' or a complete code of life based on the Qur'an and the Sunna of Mohammad.

With regard to Judaism, we read also the command in Leviticus:

> You shall love your neighbour as yourself (19:18) [and furthermore] You shall not oppress the stranger... instead you shall love him as yourself, for you were once strangers in the land of Egypt.
>
> *(19: 33–4)*

In this respect, Sacks (2004) refers to the 'covenant' and describes it as the civil togetherness of people (not based on contract or the pursuit of self-interest) within which people recognise their obligation to respond to one another beyond the letter of the law.

It is important to note that these modes of living, intrinsic to each of the major religions and defining one's relations with others, are seen to be in need of careful nurturing and formation, particularly since they contrast with the pursuit of self-interest which seems to dominate social and economic life. The Jewish covenant, according to Sacks, replaces the social contract which shapes so much political philosophy, and articulated powerfully by Thomas Hobbes' *Leviathan* in 1651. As Sacks (p. 180) explains:

> A covenant is maintained by an internalised sense of identity, kinship, loyalty, obligation, responsibility and reciprocity. These promptings cannot always be taken for granted and have to be carefully nurtured and sustained. Hence, the centrality within covenantal associations, of education, ritual, sacred narratives, and collective ceremony.

However, there is a connection between religious and moral awareness in a profounder sense than the precepts of appropriate behaviour that are part of the teaching of different religions.

First, there arises a deeper awareness of one's unworthiness, which grows with religious consciousness, and of the need for redemption – beyond what can be achieved through purely human words and actions. In taking religion seriously, one comes to think differently about what one ought to do (the duties which make demands upon one) and how one is disposed to live (for example, the virtues, such as humility, which dispose one to act in particular ways in particular situations). This is expressed thus in the Epistle of St. James:

> If any man thinketh himself to be religious, while he bridleth not his tongue but deceiveth his heart, this man's religion is vain. Pure religion and undefiled before our God and Father is this, to visit the fatherless and widows in their affliction, and to keep himself unspotted from the world.

Second, however, that 'examined life' might logically seek (as argued by Kant) the principle to which there would be ultimate appeal – in so acting

> as to treat humanity, whether in your own person or in that of any other, always at the same time as an end, and never merely as a means.

Such a principle might partly be seen as the pursuit of happiness, but a recognition of the worth of other people's deserving of such happiness as expressed in the appropriate feelings and virtues (for example, tenderness, caring, forgiveness) – but also pursuing, either through personal initiatives or through social and political means, justice and the 'common good'. Such an ideal provides a further challenge for religious education in schools, as will be argued in Chapter 9.

But here the religious dimension can make an entry, since that happiness might be seen, as it was for St. Augustine, as a relationship with God as the source of all creation. In arguing for this, St. Augustine was of course speaking from within a Neoplatonic tradition of philosophising, in which there is a gradual assent to God through thought, prayer, actions and relationships – an 'examined life' which leads to the postulation of the source of all life and of what constitutes the satisfaction and happiness sought. Hence, according to St. Augustine,

> ethics are here, since a good and honest life is not formed otherwise than by loving as they should be loved those things which we ought to have, namely, God and our neighbour.
>
> *(quoted in Copleston, 1950, p. 82)*

To achieve this one needs to follow the appropriate moral rules (embedded in our consciences) and develop the appropriate dispositions and virtues, which is greatly aided by the narratives within the different religious traditions.

Conclusion

Faith concerns the beliefs in a divine reality – in there being a God (responsible for the phenomenal world) and in a way of living in relationship to God. Such beliefs arise, as argued in the previous chapters, from many different strands of evidence, making those beliefs 'reasonable', if not proven in the strict sense.

One such strand of evidence lies in the imperative nature of moral thinking, reflected in the strong sense of duty and obligation and in the dictates of conscience, in contrast, say, to the pursuit of self-interest. There would seem to be, as Newman argued (and quoted above),

> a relation between the soul and a something exterior, and that moreover superior, to itself; a relation to an excellence which it does not possess, and to a tribunal over which it has no power.

The religious person would no doubt feel the will of God in the promptings of conscience. A 'challenge' for religious education, therefore, as will be enlarged upon in Chapter 9, must be this formation of conscience – of making explicit the maxims from which one is acting and of subjecting such maxims to the 'universalisation principle' as posed by Kant. Would one be prepared to promote the maxims, which are implicit in so acting, to other people's actions and choices?

Furthermore, having 'a faith', as witnessed in the major Abrahamic religions, both entails and is enhanced by a way of life which is characterised by moral principles, central to which are the care and love for other human beings, living in harmony within the wider society.

To be 'fully human', therefore (which was the opening query of this chapter), would require, first, this relationship with God (reflected in a way of life through liturgies and rituals and through respecting the ethical demands which are laid down in the Scriptures, the Torah and the Qur'an and Sunna) and through the relationship with fellow human beings (reflected not only in the consciousness of moral rules but also in the exercise of the virtues).

This sense of 'being fully human' and, in consequence, seeking the 'common good' (with special regard for the poor and disadvantaged) gives rise to a further challenge for religious education in schools, as related in final Chapter 9.

Bibliography

Ayer, A.J., 1936, *Language, Truth and Logic*, Harmondsworth: Penguin.
Copleston, F., 1950, *A History of Philosophy*, vol. II, London: Burns Oates and Washbourne.
Harries, R., 2002, *God Outside the Box*, London: SPCK.
Hobbes, T., 1651, *Leviathan*.
Hume, D., 1751, *Inquiry concerning Principles of Morals*.
Kant, I., 1783, *Prolegomena to any Future Metaphysic*.
Kant, I., 1785, *Groundwork of the Metaphysics of Morals*.
Kant, I., 1788, *Critique of Practical Reason*.
Kant, I., 1797, *The Metaphysics of Morals*.
Leo XIII, 1875, *Rerum Novarum*, Vatican.
MacIntyre, A., 2009, *God, Philosophy, Universities*, London: Continuum.
Newman, J.H., 1826/1843, *Sermons Preached Before the University of Oxford* (quoted in MacIntyre, 2009, p. 141).
Oakeshott, M., 1933, *Experience and its Modes*, Cambridge University Press.
Plato, *Apology* 38a5–6.
Sacks, J., 2004, 'Political society, civil society', in Haldane, J., ed., *Values, Education and the Human World*, Exeter: Imprint Academic.
Sartre, 1959, *Existentialism and Humanism*, London: Methuen.
Strom, M.S., 1981, 'Facing history and ourselves: Integrating a holocaust unit into the curriculum', New York: Moral Education Forum (Summer 1981).
United Nations, 1966a, *Conventions on Civil and Political Rights*.
United Nations, 1966b, *Convention on Social, Cultural and Economic Rights*.

6
SPIRITUAL DEVELOPMENT

In speaking of the moral dimension to religious faith and practice (namely, with reference to virtues and duties, and to responses to the voice of conscience), there is still something missing, which is reflected in the lives of those who are singled out as exemplars of religious living, namely, that which 'inspires them'. That 'something' is captured in the idea of the 'spiritual'. But that word is used so loosely (as reflected in Chapter 1) that there is need to define and explain its distinctiveness, especially within a religious and moral tradition such that its development should be one of the challenges for religious education (see Chapter 9).

In retrospect

Chapter 1 indicated that, as commitment to a distinctive religious *faith* declined in the development and concept of religious education (detailed figures are given in Chapter 8 on the rise of the secular society), there became an increasing emphasis (for example, in the 1944 and the 1988 Education Acts, and in official recommendations such as those of the 1993 NCC, entitled *Spiritual and Moral Development*) on 'spiritual development'. This, however, was very widely understood in order to embrace a range of practices and beliefs and not to be identified with a specific religious understanding. Thus, spirituality was seen to do with 'relationships with other people and, *for believers*, with God'. It includes

> the universal search for individual identity [and] the search for meaning and purpose in life and for the values by which to live.

But such a search for 'individual identity' and for 'the values by which to live' brings it into the sphere of moral education, as described in the previous chapter, and, thereafter for many, into the distinctively religious sphere of discourse.

70 Spiritual development

In giving the concept such a broad application, however, it must not be thought that the word was necessarily and always used equivocally (as that word was explained in Chapter 3). Its different uses might be seen to have a common heritage, namely, a quality of living and of aspiration which transcends purely material interests and motivation. But even here one would want to distinguish (as Gill and Thomson do in the General Introduction to their edited book, Redefining Religious Education: spirituality for human flourishing, p. 6) between 'thinner' and 'thicker' conceptions of the word – and yet examine a continuum between them.

This is important to acknowledge (and, I suspect, frequently is not acknowledged in the 'Challenges for Religious Education', as recounted in Chapter 9 of this book). For if there is a continuum between 'thinner' and 'thicker' meanings, then that 'thicker meaning', as embodied in a religious form of life, might emerge through relevant, but not initially religious, experiences into a more profound spiritual understanding, opening up a possible religious interpretation. Chapter 2 referred to the impact which the sight of Tintern Abbey had upon William Wordsworth. It was an aesthetic experience of a great moment, but it pointed beyond the purely aesthetic to a different realm of being – to the source of such beauty. Hence, the connection is made possible between the increasing spiritual awareness and the possibility of a religious dimension to our search for meaning. The 'thin sense of spiritual' merges into a much thicker one!

Linking the spiritual with the theological – practice with reason

Therefore, what could be referred to, at least initially, as a 'subjective state of mind', might indicate, and lead on to, the 'postulation' of a presence which transcends the phenomenal world and which comes to be embodied in a 'form of life'. It is the latter which is the focus of this chapter, namely, an understanding of spirituality (as that might develop in each person) as intrinsic to religious understanding and thereby essential to religious formation and to religious education. Indeed, to many it is not possible to separate the two, namely, the understanding of religion and its beliefs, on the one hand, and, on the other, the distinctive form of life intrinsic to such understanding. As Sheldrake (1998) announces in the opening chapter of *Spirituality and Theology*, expressing the dependence of theology on spiritual experience,

> A theology that is alive is always grounded in spiritual experience. If it is to be complete, theology needs to be *lived* just as much as it needs to be studied and explained.
>
> (p. 3)

And thus, elsewhere (p. 32),

> Theology ... needs the correction of spirituality to remind us that the true knowledge of God concerns the heart as much as the intellect.

In so saying, Sheldrake follows no less an authority than St. Augustine:

> God is known not by 'scientia' but by 'sapienza' – that is to say, not by objectification and analysis but by a contemplative knowledge of love and desire.
> *(De Trinitate, Book XII-XIV)*

On the other hand, according to Sheldrake, as he points to that intrinsic link between spirituality and theology, just as the latter is empty without the former, so 'spirituality without theology runs the danger of becoming private or interior' – a purely subjective state of mind.

What therefore is important for religious education must be this close, indeed logical, connection between belief (enlivened by appropriate feelings) and practice. However, such a position goes against the assumptions inherited from the 'Enlightenment' (as described in Chapter 3) in which reason, and thus reasonableness, and the search for understanding are to be divorced from feelings which, though permeating our responses to the world, are seen to obviate 'knowledge'. But as we saw from Chapter 2, that sense of the divine, leading to faith, may be deeply rooted (to use Pascal's words) in the 'reasons of the heart'.

On the other hand, as indicated in Chapters 3 and 4, the purely rational basis for believing in God does not lead to knowledge *about* God and thus to a way of life permeated by such knowledge. However, such a rational basis gives rise to an indication of some Transcendent Being, who, however, in purely rational terms, remains ineffable. Theology as an intellectual discipline can go only so far. Theology, however, signals what might be understood more personally of that Transcendent Being within major religious traditions – for example, within Christianity, the physical presence of the incarnate God disclosed through Jesus Christ. One sees, too, that struggle through the Old Testament to articulate in concrete terms what the prophet Isaiah referred to as that which is 'disguised in majesty and mystery'.

In each religious tradition that divine presence is increasingly appreciated and articulated through a life of prayer, ritual and worship, as is shown through the lives and practices of those who are traditionally seen to be exemplars of life lived religiously. Practice embodies faith, and faith becomes more intelligible through the evolved practices, subject to theological critique and interpretation. Such 'living religiously' – the mutual and reciprocal relationship of thought and of feeling, of desire for fulfilment and of theological critique – would be referred to as living a spiritual life, not reduced to merely material pleasure and understanding.

All this might be best understood if we were to work through examples, but (back to Sheldrake's quotes above) such spirituality at the heart of religious beliefs must reflect a way of life which enhances religious understanding and at the same

72 Spiritual development

time be disciplined by the theological understanding. Not any sort of 'spiritual experience' would be acceptable.

Examples

An Islamic perspective

Seyyed Hossein Nasr (1987, p. 195), in a final chapter entitled, 'The Spiritual Message of Islamic Art', states that

> The sacred art of Islam is, like all veritable sacred art, a descent of heavenly reality upon earth. It is the crystallisation of the spirit and form of Islamic revelation dressed in the robe of a perfection which is not of this world of corruption and death.

That Islamic revelation did, of course, give a detailed account of the way of life which was to be incumbent on all Muslims and made available through the Shari'a, namely, a clear and well-defined path which leads to that life in accordance with the will of God. That path is embodied in the Five Pillars of Islam, as revealed in the Qur'an. They provide that daily awareness of God and of one's way of living within the spirit of Islam, namely,

- professing and practising the principal beliefs of Islam,
- ritual prayer five times a day,
- giving of one's wealth to the poor ('zakat'),
- fasting during the month of Ramadan,
- making the pilgrimage ('Hajj') to Mecca at least once in a lifetime.

Within Islam ('Islam' meaning the state of perfect harmony between God and all creation), through the books of guidance (the Qur'an and the 'Sunna', meaning a pattern of behaviour that the people should follow), the followers of Islam have been called to live an ethical life following the revealed will of God. Hence, the key importance of the 'Shari'a', namely 'a pathway' or a complete code of life based on the Qur'an and the Sunna of Mohammad, the spirit which lies behind the Five Pillars of Islam.

But back to the traditional art within such a spiritual tradition, because it is not a sort of afterthought but an integral manifestation of the Islamic spirit. As Nasr asks (p. 3),

> What is the origin of this art and the nature of this unifying principle whose dazzling effect can hardly be denied? Whether in the great court of the Delhi Mosque or the Qarawihyin in Fez, one feels oneself in the same artistic and spiritual universe despite all the local variations in material, structural techniques, and the like.

It is the unitary nature of this distinctive and inspiring art, across centuries and across the world (whether in calligraphy or in the structure of buildings – particularly mosques – or in the design of gardens) which relates to a 'world view' – one embodying the distinctive spiritual revelation found in the Qur'an.

A liberal Christian perspective

In the chapter entitled 'A hunger for God', Canon Brian Mountford (2003), when Vicar of St. Mary's University Church, Oxford, speaks of

> The natural human craving for meaning and purpose that motivates the search for God – the hunger for something ultimately worthwhile and of eternal value amid all the vicissitudes of life.
>
> *(p. 15)*

What are 'ultimately worthwhile' (namely, the values which are sought and, when found, direct our lives – have a reality independent of our 'imperfect and untidy lives' (reflecting what was argued in Chapter 5 on moral education where a person, in following the 'advice' of Socrates, sees that 'the unexamined life is not worth living'). But that feeling that there is something which transcends our mortal understanding, but which shapes our admiration, breaks out in remarkable ways, as illustrated by Mountford. He points, for instance, to the public reaction to the death of Princess Diana in 1997, when as much as £25 million was spent on flowers to lay at her shrines accompanied by messages of sympathy, devotion and admiration for her goodness. She had become 'an icon' – a vivid and unique symbol of what was to be admired. Was this not, asks Mountford, 'evidence of mass spiritual searching'?

North American indigenous peoples' perspective

In his contribution to the book (edited by Gill and Thomson, referred to above), Don Trent Jacob (indigenously known as 'Four Arrows') provides an account of 'the spiritual' (in a contribution interestingly entitled, *Seven indigenous spiritual principles for guiding all students towards survival, peace, health and happiness*) which, though in one sense arising from a distinctive way of life, is recognisable to those who do not participate in that social and economic context. As stated in the introduction, the religion of the Indigenous Peoples

> involves acceptance of the great mysteries of life and the appreciation of the interconnectedness of everything in the universe, including the sacredness of natural places such as ponds and parks.
>
> *(p. 88)*

Such a basic vision was summarised by Four Arrows (Don Trent Jacob) in terms of seven principles which would shape the education of the students in school, though none of these principles would be seen by the indigenous peoples as distinctively religious in the sense of commitment to a God to be worshipped. These spiritual principles might be summarised as:

- appreciation of the mysteriousness of life and yet awareness of the interconnectedness of everything in the universe – all appreciated with a sense of awe;
- respect for all creatures (not just human beings) as equally significant in this interconnectedness of everything;
- celebration of this mysteriousness and interconnectedness of everything through ceremonies, dances, songs and stories, which ensure the continuation of inherited values;
- sacredness of the environment and of distinctive places within it, and thus the importance of harmony with the different aspects of that environment;
- balanced life between different elements, eschewing dominance of one element over another (humans over nature, men over women, one people or tribe over another);
- importance of the virtues of courage (in order to put into effect the principles when they raise difficulties) and of generosity;
- (and most importantly) deep and constant reflection on 'lived experience' in which each develops a distinctive way to pursue his or her life.

Yet, despite the resonance of such 'acceptance' (or possibly because of the power of such spiritual commitment and form of life), American Indian spiritual practices were made illegal from 1892 until as late as the American Indian Religious Freedom Act in 1972.

A Christian spirituality: Saint Ignatius of Loyola

Saint Ignatius of Loyola is renowned for many things, but above all for the establishment of the Jesuit Religious Order. Those joining the Jesuits had to be 'tested out' through undergoing Ignatius' *Spiritual Exercises*. These might be summarised as follows:

- time must be spent on reflecting deeply on one's own weaknesses and sinfulness – for example, the failure to follow the calls of Christ;
- duly humbled, one dwells for some time on the changes which thereby need to take place – the bad habits to be overcome, the positive moves to be undertaken (within the community, say), and the bad motives which too often lead one astray;
- (calling upon a distinctive religious understanding) participation is required in the passion of Christ;
- (the fourth stage of the Spiritual Exercises) the hope and the determination to live a better life – in the case of the Spiritual Exercises, a life made possible through the Resurrection of Christ.

Such an account of *Spiritual Exercises* has a distinctive and detailed background, tied as it is to the life and mission of Christ as it is portrayed in the Scriptures and then in traditions of the Church. But one can easily extract from such an account (and, may I say, the few words are an exceedingly short synopsis of two or more thousand) to have an idea of what one means by a 'spiritual life' as integral to any religious knowledge and religious formation: the awareness of one's failures to live up to an ideal, the vision of that ideal and thus the person one would wish to become, the embodiment of that ideal in a way of life to be followed (as, for example, in Thomas Kempis' *Imitation of Christ*), and the systematic attempts to overcome the failures and the difficulties encountered upon the way.

Furthermore, such a staged account of spiritual endeavour and way of life might be sufficiently generic to apply across different religious traditions and indeed the spirituality claimed by those of the 'humanist faith'. As shall be argued in Chapter 9 concerning the challenges for the teaching of religious education, such an understanding of 'spiritual formation' or 'way of life' would provide a basis for positive sharing of ideas between students of different religious groups, as well as those of none.

Spiritual life within religious contexts

Such accounts, as given above, need a sharp focus – an attempt to spell out criteria by which experiences (frequently referred to as 'spiritual') might be recognised as religiously significant, constituting a distinctive 'form of life'.

First, the spiritual aspect or dimension of living one's faith would need to resonate with ordinary human feelings and aspirations – that is, being meaningful, even to those without the same convictions, by connecting with ordinary hopes and fears, loves and aspirations, but providing a vision of how life might be fruitfully lived, even if the intellectual conviction is yet lacking.

Second, (and here we return to the connection between spirituality and theology) the spiritual vision and way of life is informed by, and open to, criticism from its roots in a theological understanding of life, as provided in the Scriptures or the Qur'an and as developed theologically over the ages through scholarship and criticism. The two – theological understanding and spiritual insight and life – are, as explained above, reciprocally related.

Third, such spiritual awareness and practice are not purely private matters, but draw their strength and significance from participation in communities in which there have developed over time distinctive practices, such as rituals and communal prayers, and distinctive modes of worship.

Fourth, it would be hard to separate a genuinely religious spiritual experience from the recognition of a form of life which is seen to be better than what is to be found in a purely material world of aspirations and values. Hence, in addressing one's attention to God as the supreme end and purpose of life, so there would inevitably be a concern for the improvement of life within the community – through, for example, caring for the sick, the elderly or those in need of care. That spiritual vision enters necessarily into one's idea of community.

Fifth, the spiritual life, as portrayed here, takes us back to that sense of the sacred as was described through various authors in the second chapter of this book – what was revealed to Pascal by 'the reasons of the heart' or to Otto in the sense of 'the holy' or to James in 'the variety of religious experience'.

Bibliography

Gill, S., and Thomson, G., eds., 2014, *Redefining Religious Education: Spirituality for Human Flourishing*, New York: Palgrave Macmillan.

Kempis, T.A., 1364/1955, *The Imitation of Christ*, London: Burns Oates.

Mountford, B., 2003, *Perfect Freedom*, John Hunt Publishing Limited.

Nasr, S.H., 1987, *Islamic Art and Spirituality*, Lahore: Suhail Academy.

NCC (National Curriculum Council), 1993, *Spiritual and Moral Development*, London: DES.

Sheldrake, P., 1998, *Spirituality and Theology: Christian Living and the Doctrine of God*, London: Darton, Longman and Todd.

7

COPING WITH DOUBT – AND THE PROBLEM OF EVIL

This chapter examines the problems arising over the role of doubt in the pursuit of these enquiries, doubt not only in the force of philosophical support for the beliefs but also arising from the attempted reconciliation of God's providence and goodness with the suffering and evil which are endemic even in a world claimed to be divinely created. This requires thoughtful analysis (going back to Chapter 3) of the relation between faith and certainty, pursued with reference to the age-old philosophical attempts (for example, Augustine, Anselm and Bonaventure to begin with) to make sense of suffering and evil within a faith tradition – an issue which surely cannot be dodged in religious education and formation.

Doubt and certainty

There is a need once again to retreat to what was said in previous chapters about the relation between evidence and conclusion. The argument so far has been that it is *reasonable* to move from the evidence, which we have, to the conclusion (tentative though it might be at first) that there is an intelligent cause of the world, as we experience it, and of the human endeavours not only to make sense of that world, but also to seek morally to make that world a better place – indeed, to participate in the divine endeavour.

But 'reasonableness, as was argued in Chapter 3, is compatible with doubt. Indeed, doubt in science, for example, is a spur to seek further evidence or to advance one's understanding of the universe, which is always open to further questioning and development. Uncertainty would seem to be central to the scientific project, albeit against a background of well-tested and well-argued beliefs. But without a measure of doubt, there would be little incentive to explore possibilities further. To repeat the saying of Karl Popper, 'knowledge grows through criticism'. Therefore, our beliefs in the existence of God, in the nature of that God and in God's redemptive work within the world have grown through constant criticism, theological explanation and philosophical clarification, as reflected as far back as Boethius' *Consolations of Philosophy* in the 5th century where he spoke of philosophy as 'the lady handmaiden of theology'. There is no pause, nor will there be, in such a search for understanding, although such a search will build on the results of what has been previously achieved, even if subsequently questioned. Doubt would seem to be intrinsic to progress.

Faith, therefore, is a combination of uncertainty (that is, the evidence for reasonableness never adding up to 'proof' in the strict sense of that word), and yet confidence. One has perused the different sorts of evidence; one has experienced the way of life (spiritual and moral) to which those different kinds of evidence lead; one has (to some extent at least), shared the experiences spoken of in Chapter 2. But doubts may never disappear entirely, just as they may well not do so amongst those who have rejected such beliefs. Reasonableness, it would seem, is compatible with a degree of uncertainty, whether for the religious believers or for the atheists and, of course, the agnostics.

Descartes' solution

The philosopher Descartes (1596–1650) is often seen as the inaugurator of modern philosophy. His life spanned a period of deeply divided claims about the truth in matters of religious belief, and the different claims would often appeal to the authority of the established Church or, following the Reformation, of opposing traditions and interpretations of the Bible. Such divisions and such appeals to authority raised in Descartes' mind the philosophical questions about the basis for claiming the truth on matters of controversy and about the grounds for truth in such claims for certainty. But such a concern for establishing the truth and the certainty of beliefs went further than the interest in religion. It embraced scientific so-called knowledge as well. How can we arbitrate even in our understanding of the physical world between different foundations for the knowledge we claim and for the further advancement of that knowledge? Was there a method by which such knowledge could be advanced and by which differences could be reconciled? And if there were not, then (except where it was *practically* necessary to do so) one should not accept the claims for knowledge and thereby the certainty of those claims as a basis for living.

The well-known method by which Descartes was to progress from doubt to certainty was that by which he doubted everything, imagining, for example, that a wicked demon was deceiving him. What he, Descartes, thought was happening could be but a dream created by the demon. But there was a logical limit to how far such radical doubt could be maintained. There was one thing he could not doubt, namely, that he, Descartes, was doubting. In the famous sentence, *Cogito, ergo sum* – I am thinking (doubting), therefore I am – Descartes had concluded with indubitable certainty that he, Descartes, existed; otherwise it would have been logically impossible to doubt his existence.

However, from here in his *Meditations*, he needed to branch out from the different kinds of mental or subjective awareness of a world to there being an external world corresponding to these mental states (that is, to those objects of which he was conscious). How do I know (can I be certain of) the actual existence of the paper on which I am writing, rather than it being but part of the dream? Indeed, how could he be certain, not just of himself as having a mind which thinks, but having a body somehow related to that mind? How possible is it to avoid what has been referred to as the 'cartesian dualism' of mind and body?

The way out of this problem for Descartes had two steps.

First, was the argument very similar to that of Saint Anselm's 'ontological argument', concerning the existence of God, which went as follows,

> God is that than which no greater can be thought.
> But that than which no greater can be thought must exist, not only mentally, in idea, but also extra-mentally.
> Therefore, God exists, not only in idea, mentally, but also extra-mentally.

The second step might be summarised by showing that such a God would not deceive and that therefore the mental awareness of the external material world (including that of one's body) must be correct. There must exist, therefore, finite material objects independent of our consciousness of them, which are but reflected in the appearances of those objects.

However, the key line in the argument is the first step which assumes 'existence' to be an attribute (alongside such attributes as 'loving' or 'powerful'). But the logical difficulties in so treating 'being' as a quality, which an object has, is one reason why St. Anselm's argument could not meet the criticism of Aquinas.

One might interject here for the sake of the bemused reader that many philosophers (including Bishop Berkeley, 1685–1753) have had to tackle the perceived problem of relating our mental images of an independently existing material world to their being a correct account of that world existing independently of our consciousness of it, cleverly reflected in Mgr. Ronald Knox's response to the idealist philosopher Berkeley, who, along with Descartes, argued that indubitable knowledge (that is, knowledge of finite material things) did not extend beyond our states of consciousness:

> There was a young man who said 'God'
> Must find it exceedingly odd
> To think that the tree
> Should continue to be
> When there's no one about in the quad.

Reply

> Dear Sir: Your astonishment's odd;
> I am always about in the quad.
> And that's why the tree
> Will continue to be
> Since observed by yours faithfully, God.

80 Coping with doubt – and the problem of evil

Somehow the explanatory power of a God could not be left out. And indeed, the doubting Descartes breaks through any doubts about God in his assertion of awe (reminiscent of that awareness of the numinous elaborated in Chapter 2 of this book), when he declares in the *Third Meditation* (final paragraph) of his discovery of God,

> Here let me pause for a while, and gaze at, wonder at, and adore the beauty of this immense light, in so far as the eye of my darkened intellect can bear it.

It is important to conclude this section, therefore, by saying that the philosophical basis for doubt is endemic in all our thinking, whether religious, scientific, interpersonal or common sense. But such a 'philosophical problem' normally fails to enter into our everyday awareness and judgments about the physical world with which we interact. However, it rightly sneaks in when we enter the interpersonal world of understanding others' motives and states of mind, and even more so when we enter the religious world of more universal explanations and modes of understanding.

Therefore, it makes sense to speak of 'degrees of doubt'.

Degrees of doubt

It is important here to dwell on the different degrees to which one might be said to be in a state of doubt. There need not be such a sharp contrast between doubt and certainty as usually supposed. Thus, Richard Dawkins in *The God Delusion* (p. 48, referred to in Kenny, 2007, p. 392) points to a range of uncertainties or depths of doubts between 'knowing that' and 'knowing not that', namely,

(i) I know there is a God.
(ii) I do not know but strongly believe.
(iii) I am uncertain but inclined to believe.
(iv) I think God's existence and non-existence equiprobable.
(v) I am uncertain but inclined to be sceptical.
(vi) I think God's existence is very improbable.
(vii) I know there is no God.

But, as Kenny (2007) points out, there are close similarities here between Dawkins' 'spectrum of doubt' and that of Thomas Aquinas, addressing the same issues in his *Summa Theologica* (II-line.2.1) – an unlikely alliance, one might think – as he moves from *scientia* (knowledge), to *opinio* (conviction), to *suspicio* (guess), to *dubitatio* (doubt).

How then does such a 'spectrum' of belief and doubt affect our understanding of 'having a faith', or affect (in anticipation of Chapter 9) the practice of deliberate formation of young people in that faith whether in home or in school?

First, it seems necessary to repeat the distinction between 'reasonableness' and 'knowledge'. Much that we believe is based on good evidence; it has arisen from debate and insight within the larger community, following a long and active tradition; it has survived thoroughgoing criticism. There is a tradition of evidence-seeking which may not lead to the certainties reflected in such judgments as, 'this world has a history going back thousands of years' (even though such a statement, depending on evidence, is not open to verification and thus 'knowledge', as defined by Ayer – (see Chapter 4). But such evidence-seeking might justifiably lead to strong and reasonable belief on which to base one's life and the formation of one's children.

Second, even if short of 'knowledge', as that might strictly be defined, one might argue that religious belief provides stronger evidence than that which supports an alternative *secular* faith and way of life (as that is to be described in Chapter 8). Furthermore, such a secular way of life, supported by a long and developing tradition of humanist thinking, has no more claim on certainty and justified conviction than has the religious. Its reasonableness, as that is argued, does not add up to knowledge where that is defined in terms of verified true beliefs. Indeed, one might say the same of any moral form of life based on firm convictions. The history of ethics (as reflected in Chapter 5) reveals differently held convictions for the basis of obligations and of the virtues to be nurtured.

The issue is clearly summed up, once again by Aquinas, no less (quoted by Kenny, op.cit. p. 394):

> The state which is belief involves a firm adhesion to one side of the question. In this a believer is in the same position as someone who has knowledge or understanding; and yet his assent is not warranted by any clear vision, so that in that respect he resembles someone who doubts, guesses or is convinced.

The argument so far, therefore, is that it is perfectly reasonable to believe in God and in God's revelation and thereby to be committed to a way of life consonant with such a belief or set of beliefs. Such a 'faith' would be the conclusion of, and sustained by, ever greater insights arising from the several different sources of faith which converge on that conclusion and which have been referred to in the earlier chapters. And yet doubts may not be diminished – indeed, might well increase, and the reasons for continuing doubts would seem to matter for the development of religious education and formation in schools. The main reasons would seem to be, first, 'neglect and forgetfulness', and, second, 'the problem of suffering and evil'.

The problem of neglect and forgetfulness

Religious faith grows through the prayerful reflection on what may at first be what one was only dimly aware of and through the spiritual and moral life which is intrinsic to the faith's tradition. But such commitment, at the basis of continuing belief, can too easily diminish where alternative ways of life (not initially or obviously assuming different and contrary beliefs) begin to permeate one's life and thinking. The secular world (to borrow the words of Charles Taylor, 2007, and developed in Chapter 8 in this book) provides 'different horizons of significance'. Such 'horizons' might well include instantaneous gratifications, economic imperialism and the undermining of those virtues (for example, of modesty, humility, caring, prayerfulness) which are intrinsic to the religious mode of living. It is so easy to seek fulfilment in the pleasures and treasures of this world and to diminish the importance of the orientation to a religious way of living which challenges the secular vision of more instant satisfaction. Intrinsic to such a transformation is the growing doubt about the relevance or persuasiveness of the religious claims upon one. The 'real assent', described by Newman, can so easily become a mere 'notional assent'. As he states in *The Grammar of Assent* (p. 105),

> It is certain, too, that, whether it [the divine image within us] grows brighter or stronger, or on the other hand is dimmed, distorted or obliterated, depends on each of us individually, and on his circumstances. It is more than probable that, in the event, from neglect, from the temptations of life, from bad companions, or from the urgency of secular occupations, the light of the soul will fade away and die out.

The problem of suffering and evil

Nonetheless, there is one ground for doubt which cannot be dismissed easily. That is the compatibility between, on the one hand, belief in God, who is both all loving and all powerful, and, on the other hand, the presence of so much suffering and evil in the world as created. As Peter Hebblethwaite said in *The Essence of Christianity*,

> The most widely given reason for atheism or loss of faith is inability to square the horrors of cruelty, war and natural disaster with belief in an all-powerful, all-loving God.

(1996, p. 71)

It is an issue which theologians and philosophers of religion (Saint Augustine in the 4th century, Saint Anselm in the 10th, St. Bonaventure in the 12th) struggled with but without easy solutions which would convince many doubters, especially the students who seriously raise such questions.

There are two dimensions to this threat to holding religious beliefs – on the one hand, the presence of 'evil' in the world arising from human purposeful activity, and, on the other hand, the presence of physical suffering not resulting from human agency.

The problem of 'evil'

Such a problem and its ground for doubt were indeed the basis of the 'Manichaean heresy' in the 4th century which claimed that there must be, apart from God, a creator (an evil deity) of whatever is deficient and evil in the universe – a heresy which was finally attacked by a converted St. Augustine. Rather was evil, in the language of early Christian philosophers and inherited from the Greek philosopher, Plotinus, a *privation* of the 'right order in the created will'. That freedom of the will laid open the possibilities either of shaping one's life in accordance with the wishes of the loving God (being part, as it were, of God's pursuit of the good life as expressed in the moral law) or of choosing one's own idea of the good life (for example, the pursuit of personal pleasure) and thereby a falling away from God. As St Augustine stated,

> Let each one question himself as to what he loveth; and he shall find of which city (Jerusalem or Babylon) he is a citizen.

See Copleston, 1950, p. 85, for the above quote and for further explanation of St. Augustine's release from Manichaeism and re-interpretation of evil as a privation of the 'right order' – a failure to pursue the good as that is embodied in the divine plan, rather than some further force in the world, which had underpinned the Manichaean heresy.

However, so many shattering events have shown the darker side of human nature – most obviously, in recent times, that of the Holocaust during the Second World War, but clearly in the horrors prevalent in the tragic rivalries in the Middle East of recent years. How can these be reconciled with an all-loving and all-powerful Creator? Just recently (indeed, as I am writing) news has come of the appalling massacre of nearly 50 Muslims at two mosques in Christ Church, New Zealand – certainly a 'privation of the right order' or a 'deviation from the moral law of God', but so gross and inexplicable in terms of the hatred displayed by the assassin that the problem of evil cannot be easily understood or explained away.

Nonetheless, despite so many attempts at such a reconciliation over the ages, it would seem necessary to fall back on the belief that evil necessarily arises from the freedom bestowed on human beings to pursue the 'good life', the life in accordance with God's will. Such a possibility of deviating from what is morally desirable would seem to be intrinsic to the dignity of human life, namely, the ability and tendency to act in accordance with the divine will as that is encapsulated in the well-informed conscience, as described in Chapter 5. Such moral attainment entails the possibility of failure – of giving way to contrary and, what immediately seem to be more desirable, courses of action. To be human is to have freedom of will, and giving way to even small temptations begins to diminish the attraction of what was seen to be good and indeed obligatory. Giving way to small temptations so easily leads to submitting to the large ones.

The 'free will defence' given by the philosopher Alvin Platinga in his paper, 'God, evil and the metaphysics of freedom', can be summarised as follows (quoted in McGrath, 2007, pp. 233/234):

> Free will is morally important. That means that a world in which human beings possess free will is superior to a hypothetical world in which they do not. If human beings were forced to do nothing but good that would

represent a denial of human free will. God must bring into being the best possible world that he is able to do. It must therefore follow that God must create a world with free will. This means that God is not responsible if human beings choose to do evil, since God is operating under self-imposed constraints that mean that God will not compel human beings to do good.

Therefore, put briefly, to be human is to have free will, the capacity to pursue the 'good life' as it is embedded in the moral law and in the virtues (as described in Chapter 5). But such freedom of will entails the possibility of rejecting such a pursuit as more immediate desires and pleasures take control. Life always involves a choice between what one ought to do and what one wants to do and thereby can arise the gradual erosion of a sense of duty and of the virtues which reflect human living at its best.

Furthermore, in an argument developed by Swinburne, 2004, in the chapter entitled, 'The Problem of Evil', the harm perpetrated by others or by the physical world provides the ongoing context in which people are able to exercise compassion and love – the *sine qua non* of the distinctively human life expounded in Chapter 5 of this book. Swinburne (2004, p. 240) encapsulates his argument (expressed at much greater length) as follows:

> The great good of compassion (the natural emotional response to the sufferings of others) can be felt only if others are suffering. It is good that we should be involved with others emotionally when they are at their worst as well as at their best.

But the doubters (particularly the students) may well ask why is so much suffering needed in order to achieve the supreme moral aim of loving one another or of showing compassion. Yet so it might be replied, according to Harries (2012, p. 161),

> Yet Christianity has always offered hope – not just hope for heaven but hope that humanity can co-operate with God in his unceasing work of trying to bring good out of evil.

Cottingham (p. 148) similarly concludes 'this hard fact that the law of love is the law of sacrifice', quoting T.S. Eliot's *Four Quartets* (lines 207–11):

> Who then devised the torment? Love.
> Love is the unfamiliar Name
> Behind the hands that wove
> The intolerable shirt of flame
> Which human power cannot remove

In other words, much suffering arises from the wrongful use of 'free will' which in turn is an essential quality of being human. At the same time, that misuse of free will creates situations in which others can exercise the virtues of being compassionate, caring and loving.

The problem of physical suffering

However, even if the above justification for the existence of human evil-doing were to be accepted, it does not apply to so much physical suffering which is clearly not caused by human agency, as when there have been devastating earthquakes, overwhelming floods or contagious diseases. This, therefore, raises different grounds for doubt. As Briggs et al., 2018, argue in their aptly entitled book, *It's Keeping Me Seeking*,

> An abiding difficulty in the facts about natural processes, for anyone who trusts in God, is the presence of so much pain. And many animals [*including human animals* – this author's insertion] have only a brief experience of life, far short of what one feels they might legitimately expect on their behalf.... It strikes a sensitive person as wrong that there should be lingering drawn-out suffering.
>
> *(p. 206–7)*

The authors (all distinguished Oxford scientists) partly explain the compatibility of this with the divine creation

> as an integral part of the processes by which the ecosphere has developed.

This, at first reading, is not very persuasive, and, since the presence of physical suffering would very likely be an objection raised by pupils as they address questions about the existence of God, it would need further justification. Perhaps, then, one needs to look at the broader context of such disasters and suffering, because, as Cottingham (2009), p. 146) reminds us, 'the problem of suffering [is]one of the most persistent obstacles to belief in God'. But, in addressing this enigma of such suffering, Cottingham (p. 147) points out that the universe, of which we are part, is and always has been the product of a constant process of decay and destruction.

> Hydrogen atoms, fused under unimaginable pressures, decay into helium – without this there would be no stars, no light, no warmth. Suns sometimes become unstable and explode in cataclysmic bursts of destruction – without this there would be no heavier elements, out of which the planets and our own bodies are made. And the process of life itself, from the cellular level to the level of organisms and even whole eco-systems, is a constant battle of energies, as animals and plants destroy each other, and in turn decay or are consumed in the ceaseless struggle for existence.

Human beings, therefore, as an integration of mind and matter, or soul and body, are necessarily part of this process and therefore necessarily subject to physical forces such as these as a condition of their very being, just as they are subject to the temptations to act against the moral commandments by the exercise of free will, which makes them distinctively human.

However, to say that people, as material as well as spiritual beings, are necessarily subject to this disintegrating process and thus to the physical sufferings which accompany it, hardly satisfies the sceptic who points to the immense sufferings which in no way can be attributed to human folly. And Swinburne's reference to suffering affecting others as a condition for the practice of virtues such as compassion and caring is not very persuasive in the light of the magnitude of so many disasters.

Conclusion

Progress in the development of faith arises from different sources as described in Chapters 2, 3, 4 and 5, and converges on conclusions, tentative maybe, which stimulate further reflection and development. But such progress is necessarily accompanied by different degrees of doubt, which stimulate yet further questioning and deepening of understanding.

Such doubts may often arise through neglect of a religious form of life in which the faith is embedded or through the dominance of the secular world with its own 'horizons of significance'. And such doubts may be overcome by the 'reasons of the heart' of which Pascal spoke (as explained in Chapter 2) and which might be deepened through the embodiment of 'the sacred' in religious ritual, or in music and the arts.

However, the doubts become more challenging when faced with the problems of human suffering and the evil which human beings inflict on each other.

The final section attempted to deal with this two-fold problem. In so doing, it went as far as it rationally could, namely, seeing physical suffering as part and parcel of being human (both mind and matter) in the ever-developing material world, and seeing human ill-treatment as a consequence of the bestowal of free will – itself a necessary feature of a moral life.

Bibliography

Aquinas, T., *Summa Theologica*, II-Iiae,2,1.
Boethius, 523, *De Consolatione of Philosophiae*.
Briggs, A., Halvorson, H., and Steane, A., 2018, *It's Keeping Me Seeking*, Oxford: Oxford University Press.
Coplestone, F., 1950, *A History of Philosophy*, vol. II, London: Burns Oates and Washbourne.
Cottingham, J., 2009, *Why Believe?* London: Continuum.
Dawkins, R., 2006, *The God Delusion*, London: Bantam Press.
Eliot, T.S., 1942, *Little Gidding, in Four Quartets*, London: Faber.
Harries, R., 2012, *God Outside the Box*, London: SPCK.
Hebblethwaite, B., 1996, *The Essence of Christianity*, London: SPCK.

Kenny, A., 2007, 'Knowledge, belief and faith', *Philosophy*, 82: 321.
McGrath, A., 2007, *Christian Theology: An Introduction*, 5th ed., Oxford: Wiley-Blackwell.
Newman, J.H., 1870/1955, *The Grammar of Assent*, Image Books.
Swinburne, R., 2004, *The Existence of God*, 2nd. ed. Oxford: Clarendon Press.
Taylor, C., 2007, *A Secular Age*, Harvard University Press.

8

SURVIVING THE SECULAR AGE?

It would be wrong to complete such an account without a wider reference to the secularisation of society which (so often either indifferent to religious belief or hostile towards it) is seen to militate against support for religious education which claims to provide distinctive ways of understanding both reality and a form of life shaped by that understanding. Certainly in the last few centuries there has developed a way of understanding reality, and the place of reason within such understanding, which would seem to undermine religious faith. That we need to explore in this chapter, which outlines the different meanings of 'secular society', points to the limitations in such conceptions and indicates a possible practical reconciliation (most important for meeting the challenges faced by religious education) in what is now commonly referred to as the 'post-secular society'.

Nietzsche and the death of God

In 1882, the German philosopher, Friedrich Nietzsche, declared 'the death of God'. Such a statement and subsequent argument both anticipated the gradual and serious decline in religious belief, certainly within Europe (see the section below for contemporary evidence), and justified why it should be so. Thus, in *Joyful Wisdom* (1882), through the words of the madman, he asks

> Where has God gone? I will tell you. We have killed him – you and I! We are all his murderers. But how have we done it? ... Who gave us the sponge to rub out the entire horizon? What were we doing when we unchained the earth from the sun? ... Where are we going? ... God is dead. God is still dead. We killed him. How are we going to cheer ourselves up, the worst of all murderers?

But

> whoever is born after us will, thanks to this deed, live in a loftier history than there has ever been.

It is important to heed two messages contained within these statements.

The first message is the assertion of a very different understanding of how we understand the world, its moral culture and each other from that of the previously dominant religious 'horizons of significance' (a phrase used by Charles Taylor, 2007). If God is dead, then the horizons would seem to be completely open, unrestricted by previous rules and demands, enabling persons to develop the sort of life they wish for, free of religious constraints. Man takes the place of God as the creator of values – in the 'will to power'. Religion is but the invention of those who are dissatisfied with the 'world of becoming' and are therefore seeking an abiding world of being. But there is no 'absolute truth', especially where issues of value and obligation are concerned. Value and obligation are not to be discovered but rather are to be created.

The second message is that such a shift in understanding leads to a 'loftier history than there has ever been', as human beings are freed from the constraints of religious beliefs and context which had restricted moral aspirations and personal fulfilment, thereby going 'beyond good and evil' as these were entrenched within those religious traditions (see Nietzsche, 1886). Thus we see portrayed by Nietzsche the 'superman', the person who, freed from all inherited moral constraints, asserts his freedom in creating the powerful person he wants to be, indeed the creator of what is to be his ultimate value – the totally autonomous being. Characteristic of such a person, therefore, is 'the will to power'. Freed from authority, whether from the authority inherited from parents or from the authority of social and religious culture, each personally decides on the life worth living. There is nothing objective (that is, independent of the will of the agent) in the values to be adopted.

Secular society in a secular world

In the light, therefore, of such a Nietzschean view and of the modification of it in much humanist thought (which will be examined in greater detail below), we need to ask what it means to refer to a society (such as that in Britain, increasingly in Ireland and in much of the Western world) as secular – or at least becoming increasingly secular, if not going the whole way with Nietzsche in portraying man as now being freed from all moral constraints. In his book, *A Secular Age*, Charles Taylor (2007) traces the gradual evolution in the meaning of 'secular' when applied to society as it reflects the changing social and cultural traditions, although what follows is this author's expansion of Taylor's account. In many respects, Nietzsche's predictions were correct but were reflected in different ways and to different degrees which briefly (and possibly a little crudely) are set out as follows.

(i) Withdrawal of reference to God in public and moral life

Taylor refers to the withdrawal of reference to God in key aspects of public life where once such reference was integral. This is sometimes very explicit, as is the case of the state schools in France, following the arguments of Emile Durkheim in his book, *Moral Education* (1961, p. 3.), where he argued for a purely secular education – one that required no reference to a God or religion in the formation of educational aims and in the justification of moral principles. In the United States, the First Amendment of the Constitution, as that was declared in 1791, guaranteed the separation of the State from religion and therefore the freedom from religious commitment in the organisation of public life and schooling. In Britain, there is not such a rigid separation, as is reflected in a religious symbolism surviving in different aspects of public life (as in the coronation of the Queen), and as reflected in the public funding of Faith Schools, although, in an increasingly vociferous pursuit of a secular state, the existence of such Faith Schools are being subjected to constant attack (see Pring, 2018a, The Future of Publicly Funded Faith Schools). And such attacks or criticism would seem to make sense as so many other aspects of public life have been secularised in the sense of 'emptied of God, or of any reference to ultimate reality' (Taylor, 2007, p. 3). In the words of Taylor (p. 2),

> As we function within various spheres of activity – economic, political, cultural, educational, professional, recreational – the norms and principles we follow, the deliberations we engage in, generally do not refer to God or to any religious beliefs; the considerations we act on are internal to the 'rationality' of each sphere.

One might offer, as an example of such a 'sphere', the world of economics, which is theoretically self-contained and wherein the pursuit of profit would seem to be the ultimate goal and unchallenged. For example, one has seen here the widespread contracting out of public services (in health, education, prisons, elderly care) to private profit-making businesses – all without the restraint of moral considerations which prevailed not long ago. However, in this first sense of the secularisation of society, this emptying of public life from reference to God and religious forms of life is quite compatible with the exercise of religion in individual lives; churches, synagogues and mosques continue to exist, though in the Western world no longer with a significant institutional impact upon the public sphere.

(ii) Religious commitment in need of justification

A second sense of secularisation of society, as a development from the first, is where belief in God and religious practice prevail (albeit in an increasing minority of the population), but where such belief and practice are increasingly seen to be 'odd' and not to be spoken about in general company (or, if so, in apologetic tones). 'Are you a believer?' (or a similar question) is asked in surprised tones. Grace before dinner at some Oxford Colleges has progressed from Latin (reflecting the liturgical language of the early Christian foundations) to English, spontaneously spoken, and now to a friendly welcome to the guests and an expression of gratitude, not to God (as traditionally in *Gratias tibi, Domine*) but to the cook. There is a 'secular atmosphere' where religious commitment is something which needs to be justified in a way that disbelief or indifference does not. Clearly, in such a secular context, the maintenance of a religious form of life of prayer and worship becomes increasingly difficult, since not in the experience of many, and inevitably poses problems for religious education whether inside or outside of Faith Schools. Certainly it places greater onus on showing the link between faith (belief and practice) and reason, not simply through the arguments as outlined in Chapters 3 and 4 of this book, which (back to Newman, 1855) may support merely 'notional assent' rather than 'real assent'. Such 'notional assent' would need to be accompanied by the moral and aesthetic experiences such as, perhaps within music and the arts, but as revealed or outlined in Chapter 2 of this book.

(iii) Decline in religious practice

There has been within Europe an increasing decline in religious belief and practice and thereby a rejection of certain moral commitments which had entered into the very structure of civil society – for example, with regard to the nature of and commitment to marriage, to the acceptance of same-sex civil partnerships, to the instability of family life as that was once assumed to be a life-long commitment, or to the pursuit of excessive wealth without public accountability.

Such a decline in belief and practice is reflected in the data provided by the latest British Social Attitudes Survey, 2018, which compares today's figures with those of 1983. Those identifying themselves as Christian declined from 66% to 38%; those claiming no religion rose from 31% to 52%; the number of Britons identifying themselves as Church of England or Anglican dropped from 40% to 14%; but, amongst adults under 24 that number is now no higher than 2%. Those claiming to be Catholic reduced from 10% to 7%. The majority of the population say that they have no religion (including 59% of Scots according to the Humanist Society of Scotland, as reported in *The Guardian*, 14th August, 2018).

Elsewhere, and in surprising places, this is also applicable. Mass attendance in Ireland, where until 1990 81% of those identifying themselves as Catholic attended Mass at least once a week, had dropped to 48% by 2011 and only 14% in the Dublin area (*The Tablet*, 13.1.17). And a recent article in *The Tablet* (*25.8.18*), entitled 'Ireland's Vanishing Church', reports

> that schools are dropping religious education, vocations are drying up and lay people are not being prepared to take more responsibility for the maintenance of parishes. The Irish Church faces a bleak future.

These figures might be seen as the indirect consequence of (or integral to) the different senses of 'secular' given above, the first two together creating an anti-religious atmosphere in that there is a quite dramatic turning away from God.

(iv) Moral nihilism

One consequence (though to a limited extent) of Nietzsche's rejection of the objective truth of moral values (as these were consequential upon religious faith), and of his reduction of what is to be valued to the autonomous striving of the liberated person, would seem to be the moral nihilism which would permeate society. What is to be valued is that which is created by the individual striving for complete independence of moral constraint. The 'death of God' would seem to lead to god-like persons, inventing what is to be regarded as worthwhile for them personally.

But one needs to be careful here. The 'death of God' in such matters gave way to the absolute importance of reason in the individual pursuit of deciding the future mode of life to be adopted. In separating the mechanistic material world from the spiritual, the body from the soul, supreme importance was attached by Descartes, for example, to the rational free will in determining the principles on which to act. And that achievement arises from

> the sense of having lived up to my dignity as a rational being which demands that I be ruled by reason.

This is quoted from Taylor, 2007, p. 130 sqq, who gives an extended account of Descartes' application of the 'rational will' to the maintenance of objective morality, something which appears in Habermas and Ratzinger's (2006) encounter with Cardinal Ratzinger, as explained below.

(v) The Enlightenment – and growth of 'modernism'

A connected sense of the secular lies not so much in the moral dimension, but, following the 'Enlightenment' and the development of Modernism as described in Chapter 3, arises from a purely scientific explanation of the universe as a whole and of the causal interaction of the physical entities within such a universe. God, therefore, became redundant in our understanding of physical events. A sense of mystery gets removed.

In summary

Therefore, the secular society in a secular age reflects, in various ways and to varying degrees: (i) the absence of reference to God and religion in public life; (ii) the need to explain and justify religious belief and practice often to a disbelieving audience; (iii) the decline in religious faith and practice; (iv) self-indulgent modes of living without reference to traditional religious and moral constraints; (v) the continuing influence of the Enlightenment and 'modernism' which omit the need to refer to a God in explaining events.

However, that gradual withdrawal of God from the background understandings of the physical and moral worlds we inhabit did (and still does) create for many a sense of loss, as is reflected in Matthew Arnold's poem, *Dover Beach,* in 1851 (quoted in Cottingham, 2009, p. 17).

> The Sea of Faith
> Was once, too, at the full, and round earth's shore

Lay like the folds of a bright girdle furl'd.
But now I only hear
Its melancholy, long, withdrawing roar,
Retreating to the breath
Of the night wind, down the vast edges drear
And naked shingles of the world.

Nonetheless, it is more complicated than that, given that the vacuum left by the decline of religious belief and practice has been accompanied by rival and more seriously thought-out options.

Humanist interpretation of the secular

Taylor, *In a Secular Age*, p. 18, states:

> The coming of modern secularity in my sense has been coterminous with the rise of a society in which for the first time in history a purely self-sufficient humanism came to be a widely available option. I mean by this a humanism accepting no final goals beyond human flourishing, nor any allegiance to anything else beyond this flourishing. Of no previous society was this true.

Such a sense of 'human flourishing', on this view, requires no reference to 'the transcendent', the reaching out to which was seen to be essential to religious faith as described in Chapter 2 of this book. Such lack of reference arose partly as a result of the 'modernism' referred to above and as described in greater detail in Chapter 3, pages 34–36. An explanation of the universe, both as a whole and in the complexity of its parts, is to be fully explained through the developments in science. There is nothing beyond such a world to which one needs to appeal for further explanation both of how things are or of how things ought to be.

However, care has to be taken about too sharp a contrast between the 'humanist world' and 'the religious', certainly at the beginning of recognisable secular humanism. The Christian duty was seen to be that of improving the lot of the people – the poor (as witness the introduction of the 'poor laws'), the infirm and the elderly. It was seen as a Christian virtue to shape the wider civil society in a more humane way (Calvin's Geneva being a prominent example) and as is made explicit in the New Testament. Human beings within a religious context could thus work out what is worthwhile for a distinctively human life, as well as being the agents for putting that into practice through civil action.

But for the humanists, such thoughts and practices could be engaged in without reference to God. Such a transformation of understanding obviously took place over much time, indeed centuries. But there would remain much in common between the more secular humanist tradition (as in John Locke's early formulation in his *Two Treatise on Government*) of a society based on mutual support for the good of the whole and the Christian humanists in the growing interest in a civil society (as reflected in the Papal Encyclical of Pope Leo XIII in 1879, *Rerum Novarum*, on 'the common good'), which would protect the interests of everyone and in which the religious bodies would be enabled to flourish as well as those without religious attachment.

Such a partial reconciliation is powerfully reflected in the encounter between the humanist philosopher, Jurgan Habermas (seen by Schuller, 2006, as the 'personification of liberal, individual and secular thinking') and the Pope-to-be, Cardinal Ratzinger (see Habermas and Ratzinger, 2006), following the harsh criticisms (from those who might be referred to as the humanist philosophers) which a papal encyclical entitled, *Reason and Faith*, prior to Ratzinger's election to the papacy, had received. What emerge from the dialogue are two kinds of justification for ethical conclusions in the recommendations for a good and just society.

The first (that from Habermas) was the emphasis on the resources of a democratic constitutional state, namely, the 'sovereign people', under the basic principle of the constitution providing an autonomous justification that all of the citizens can rationally accept and implement through participation and communication all oriented to the 'common good'. A social bond is thus developed.

The second justification (that of Ratzinger) agrees that secularisation, therefore, might be seen in a more positive light (than is suggested by the Nietzschean 'will to power') within the increasing influence of the secular humanism, wherein what is morally right (the development of the good of the whole, based on arrangements for mutual support) can and should be reached by reason, not necessarily by religious authority. In the words of Nietzsche, it would seem that we are open then to a 'loftier history than there has ever been'.

Therefore, 'moral seriousness' would seem to prevail within humanist traditions of different kinds (many were those, like St. Thomas More, who were described as Christian humanists), and reference might thus be made to such ancient 'humanist saints' as Cicero, Cato, Seneca and Marcus Aurelius, who proclaimed detachment from earthly ties.

However, tensions between religious and non-religious humanism inevitably gave rise to oppositions. Certainly such a tension long prevailed in France where, following the reforms of Guizot in 1833, a purely secular education was introduced within the State system of schooling, as outlined by Durkheim (1961, p. 71) in his book, *Moral Education*, where he stated,

> The last twenty years in France have seen a great educational revolution which was latent and half realised before then. We decided to give our children in our state-supported schools a purely secular education,

that is an education

> not derived from revealed religion, but that rests exclusively on ideas, sentiments and practices *accountable to reason alone* – in short a purely rationalist education.

Therefore, the 'secular' in many respects came to signify more than indifference, but instead a rational approach to understanding and pursuing the civic and moral good, rather than drawing upon religion.

Similarly, for example, the Secular Education League, formed in England in 1907, insisted that the teaching of religion was not the responsibility of the State, and indeed that the State should not be funding schools which supported religious faiths. It was within that spirit that the School Board schools were conceived. But, in so conceiving them, the secularists and subsequent humanists were not faithful to the extreme Nietzsche conclusion of the new superman freed from *all* moral constraints. Rather did they argue strongly against a morality and public life which are shaped and constrained or determined by religious beliefs. This has led many within the humanist movement to campaign against the State's support for Faith Schools (Humanist Philosophers Group, 2001, Religious Schools: the case against).

A secular tradition

There has, therefore, slowly evolved a secular tradition affecting public life in general and commitments to education in particular. Such a tradition is a socially inherited way of thinking which shapes how one sees and understands things, responds to them morally and enables one to engage with other people who share that tradition. It is what Charles Taylor (2007, p. 323) refers to as

> the generally shared background of understandings of society, which make it possible to function as it does.

A religious tradition, for example, such as Christianity, incorporates specific beliefs concerning the divinity of Christ, his establishment of a community or Church, particular practices and moral obligations, a sacramental form of life, and much more. By becoming a Christian one submits to a particular mode of thinking and behaving – one comes to see the world in a different way. But such a tradition (a 'faith', as that is described in Chapter 2) does also contain the mechanisms for its own self-criticism. The 'faith' has developed over the centuries through systematic and philosophical critique. Indeed, the possibility and the methods of such a critique are themselves part of that very tradition.

There is, in this respect, some similarity between secular and religious traditions. Both embody a 'faith' about 'human flourishing' which makes certain assumptions concerning the place of reason in determining in what exactly such flourishing consists. But those in the secular tradition do so without reference to religious belief or practice, even though much of what is contained therein is shared with religious belief and indeed has historically arisen in close conjunction with it. Indeed, the one may gain from the insights of the other. The American Declaration of Independence in 1789 may have been seen (and so expressed) as the establishment of a social order in keeping with God's designs. But the key elements in the Declaration, in what has been referred to by Taylor (p. 447) as the Modern Moral

Order, concern the association of 'disembedded individuals' coming together in association so that 'each, in pursuing his or her own purposes in life, acts to benefit others mutually'. This then now becomes a moral ideal widely shared, reached by a rationalist ideal of building an ethical basis for human living, but expressing, too (for those who want it), the religious understanding of the significance and dignity of each individual. It is here, I think, that we come to see the central factor in the difference between the religious and the secular visions in education.

On being a person

There is a danger in the secular tradition (bereft of the religious framework) which is reflected in Habermas' account (op.cit. p. 35) under the sub-title, 'When the societal bond breaks'. He refers to the external threats which threaten

> the democratic bond and exhaust the kind of solidarity that the democratic state needs but cannot impose by law.

This arises from the dynamic of the global economy and the global society and thus

> the transformation of the citizens of prosperous and peaceful liberal societies into isolated monads acting on the basis of their own self-interest, persons who used their subjective rights only as weapons against each other.

Rather it is the case that central to the good of society as a whole and thereby of each of the members of the society (an aim of both humanist and religious ethics) must be the respect for each individual as a person (not as an 'isolated monad') who is worthy of such respect and to be treated as 'an end' rather than simply as 'a means to an end'. Part, however, of the secularisation of society and the effort to seek the good of the whole has been a 'depersonalisation' of the very people whose welfare should be enhanced by that society, making the aspiration of 'human flourishing' look philosophically somewhat thin. The very language has changed.

This is particularly apparent in schooling. For example, the raising of standards and the achievement of the 'effective schools' are seen as main objectives for the public good. But this in turn has given birth to the new managerial language of 'deliverology'. This new language shapes both political discourse about educational standards and educational practice. Essential to the 'effective school' is agreement on precise *targets*. There need to be *performance indicators*, so that we know whether those targets have been hit, and regular *audits* to check that the *inputs* for attaining the *outputs* have been adopted and *delivered* by the *workforce* (who are referred to as *delivering* the curriculum).

It is a small step to see the learners or their parents as the *customers* or *clients*, choosing a particular commodity within a system increasingly seen as a *market*, in which there are schools competing for *custom*, and in which parents (the fortunate ones) exercise choice based on the *audits* of the respective schools. The White

Paper, entitled *21st Century Schools: your child, your schools, our future: building a 21st century schools system* (DCSF, 2008), referred to 'performance' and 'performing' 121 times, 'outcomes' 55 times, 'delivery' 57 times, and 'books' only once.

Here we see, in the new language created within the secularisation of society, a denial of 'the personal' in the rational pursuit of the common good. To be a person is to be something very different from a material and inanimate object such that the language and consequent treatment of the one is inappropriate for the other. A main thrust of John Macmurray's philosophy, as it was developed through his Gifford Lectures (1957 to 1961), is that the difference is much greater than is appreciated and is currently being built into our relationships and institutions. The warnings, which permeate his writing of the failure to recognise the 'personal' within a more secular society, could well have had in mind the dangers of the Orwellian newspeak which has now entered educational and social policy and practice.

No doubt such an account would be regarded as unfair by many humanists, who are equally concerned about the personal welfare of the young people as embodied in a profound respect for them as persons – as 'ends in themselves'. But my criticism is not of such people, but of an evolving tradition, affecting both humanists and religious, in which the sense of the 'personal' has been removed and the 'persons' are increasingly treated as objects serving external ends.

On the other hand, within a religious tradition such as Christianity, the concept of 'person' would or should permeate every aspect of life – through communication by prayer with the *person* of Christ and through the sacraments and the biblical texts. One can say the same thing about Judaism and Islam, and about the many unbelievers who might well cherish strong personal attachments to family and friends and who might similarly begrudge the denial of the 'personal' in the increasingly bureaucratic language of administration and control within the more secular society.

Interim conclusion: entering the post-secular society

It is frequently asserted, therefore, that we now live in a secular society, that is, a society whose way of living and whose pervasive understandings of the good and worthwhile life (indeed, whose 'horizons of significance') require no reference to religious beliefs and practices. In such a society, where such traditions persist, it becomes much less easy to maintain a truly religious ethos.

However, as developed in the beginning of the chapter, there are different (though frequently connected) meanings of 'secular' and thus 'secular society', which are imbibed by its members and which inevitably affect peoples' understanding and approach to religion and to the religious forms of life.

At one level there is but ignorance and lack of awareness of religion and a religious form of life. It no longer enters into the consciousness of many people, and this is reflected in the dramatic fall in religious practice.

At another level, there is hostility to what is seen as a hindrance to life 'in a loftier history than there has ever been'. A secular age, for example, requires a secular education, according to Durkheim, and therefore one sees the increasing hostility to faith-based schools, especially within the State system.

However, at a final level, one sees the rescue attempt by the humanists (exemplified by Habermas) through arguing how systematic reasoning, embodied in constitutional laws which encapsulate the general good, can provide the ethical basis for a person-centred society. But even here, as Habermas feels it necessary to admit, one can see how, in the absence of an ethical basis once provided by religious beliefs, there has developed a different sort of society – one which, dominated by the impersonal language of management, does not conceive persons as worthy of respect (as ends in themselves) but constructs them as objects to be manipulated (as means to ends not of their choosing). As Habermas (2010, p. 73) concludes,

> The moral sensitivity to the unjust distribution of life opportunity has by no means diminished in societies of our type.

In that respect, reference is made to how

> the imperatives of the market in the guise of cost-benefit analysis or competition permeate ever more spheres of public life [as described above with reference to education] and force individuals to adopt an objectivising standpoint in their dealings with one another.

As Ratzinger (2006) argues in his earlier response to Habermas, such reasoning is defined within the civic state and fails to comprehend the global trans-national or inter-cultural needs which today are so vital. Must there not be recourse to something beyond the constitutional and democratic agreements of the truly democratic state, namely, a 'natural law' based on the aspirations of, and consequences for, human beings as such and in reference to which the particular laws and sovereignty of conflicting societies might be judged – as now is embodied in the United Nation's Declaration of Human Rights, recognising the supreme importance of each individual?

Any tradition embodies values and modes of judgment which are not necessarily explicit in the consequent thinking and behaving of those who have inherited it. And it is important educationally to enable the learners to see this and to recognise the assumptions, especially the ethical ones which underpin their respective values and outlooks. That is the case (most important for the argument of this book) with those who follow all-embracing religious views of the world and of human destiny. However, it is equally the case with those who, in pursuit of a secular ideal, reject a religiously comprehensive pictures of the universe. Their values, modes of judgment and practical habits of behaviour have themselves been internalised through living within a secular community whose members participate in that tradition and where possibly an underlying materialism affects their judgment.

In the conclusion, therefore, of the Ratzinger/Habermas encounter, Ratzinger (p. 77) states,

I am in broad agreement with Jurgen Habermas' remarks about a post-secular society, about the willingness to learn from each other, and about self-limitation on both sides.

Habermas (2010, pp. 18, 19), in turn, recognises the role of religion in the pursuit of the secular ideal. That secular ideal would seem to depend (with reference to Kant) on the presuppositions of 'practical reason',

> which provides justifications for the universalistic and egalitarian concepts of morality and law which shape the freedom of the individual and interpersonal relations in a normatively plausible way. However, the decision to engage in action based on solidarity when faced with threats which can be averted only by collective efforts calls for more than insight into good reasons.

That 'more' would, it seems, be assisted by the assurances and images preserved by religion with its 'collectively binding ideals'. But more than that, as responded by Briekskorn (2010, pp. 27, 28), what is missing in Habermas' commitment to 'the highest reason' and yet is integral to the presuppositions of Kant's idea of 'practical and universalistic reason', is the dimension of 'transcendence' – the invocation of that which is beyond the 'freely reached consensus of free citizens'.

Therefore, reason plays an essential role in both the secular and the religious justifications of their respective positions, which has warranted the shift in title from the 'secular' to the 'post-secular' age.

Bibliography

Briekskorn, N., 2010, 'On the attempts to recall a relationship', in J. Habermas and J. Ratzinger, 2006, eds., *The Dialectics of Secularisation*, San Francisco: Ignatius Press.
Cottingham, J., 2009, *Why Believe?* London: Continuum.
CRE (Commission on Religious Education), 2017, *Religious Education for All*, London: Religious Education Council for England and Wales.
DCSF, 2008, (White Paper) *20th Century Schools: Your Child, Your Schools, Our Future: Building a 21st Century School System*, London: DCSF.
Durkheim, E., 1961, *Moral Education: A Study in the Theory and Application of the Sociology of Education*, 3rd ed., New York: The Free Press.
Habermas, J., 2010, *An Awareness of What Is Missing: Faith and Reason in a Secular Age*, Polity Press.
Habermas, J., and Ratzinger, J., 2006, *The Dialectics of Secularisation: On Reason and Religion*, San Francisco: Ignatius Press.
Halstead, M., 1995, 'Voluntary apartheid?' *Journal of Philosophy of Education*, 29 (2).
Humanist Philosophers Group, 2001, *Religious Schools: The Case Against*, London: BHA.
John, P., II, 1998, *Fides et Ratio*, Vatican Press.
Kant, I., 1788, *Critique of Practical Reason*, vol. 122.
Leo XIII, 1879, *Encyclical: Rerum Novarum*, Vatican.
Locke, J., 1690, *Two Treatises of Civil Government*.
MacMurray, J., 1957, *The Self as Agent*, London: Humanities Press International.

MacMurray, J., 1961, *Persons in Relation*, London: Humanities Press International.
Newman, J.H., 1855, *Grammar of Assent*, New York: Image Books, 1955 edition.
Nietzsche, F., 1882/1996, *Joyful Wisdom*, New York: Random House.
Nietzsche, F., 1886/1996, *Beyond Good and Evil*, New York: Random House.
Pring, R., 2018a, *The Future of Publicly Funded Faith Schools*, London: Routledge.
Pring, R., 2018b, (i), 'What counts as an educated person?' in *Thinking Philosophically About Education,* London: Routledge.
Pring, R., 2018b, (ii), 'Putting persons back into education', in *Thinking Philosophically About Education*, London: Routledge.
Ravitch, D., 2010, *The Death and Life of the Great American School System*, New York: Basic Books.
Schuller, F., 2006, '*Foreword*' to Habermas and Ratzinger, in J. Habermas and J. Ratzinger, 2006, eds., *The Dialectics of Secularisation,* San Francisco: Ignatius Press.
Taylor, C., 2007, *A Secular Age*, Harvard University Press.
White, J., 2002, 'Education and personal well-being in a secular universe', in *The Child's Mind*, Routledge.

9
THE CHALLENGES FOR RELIGIOUS EDUCATION

This penultimate chapter, following earlier chapters on the reasonableness of religious belief, identifies consequent challenges for religious education and formation in schools, both those not formally connected to a religious faith and those which are. First, how might religious education, though in no way intending to lead to religious formation, lead to understanding the truth claims and reasonableness of so believing? Second, how, on the other hand, might the reasonableness of religious faith be such that it provides a basis and justification for 'religious formation' through the acquisition of religious faith? Therefore, the challenges are shown to be somewhat different in Faith Schools from those in Community Schools which cater to pupils from several faiths or none. The challenges identified are as follows:

For non-religiously affiliated schools:

(i) understanding and appreciating 'the numinous and the sacred' which inspire the religious outlook (with particular reference to Chapter 2);
(ii) philosophical engagement with the meaning of such understanding and appreciation (with particular reference to Chapters 3 and 4);
(iii) learning from different faiths within the community (with particular reference to Chapters 2 and 4);
(iv) appreciating the moral dimension to life and the formation of conscience (with particular reference to Chapters 5 and 6);
(v) responding to the secular ethos, that is the 'horizons of significance' within society (with particular reference to Chapter 8);
(vi) finding the teachers!

For religiously affiliated (Faith) schools: (i) to (vi) above, plus:

(vii) appreciating and responding to an 'ideal' which shapes religious formation (with reference to Chapters 2, 5 and 6);

102 The challenges for religious education

(viii) *formation of social consciousness, shaped by the ideal (see Chapters 5 and 6);*
(ix) *developing 'religious literacy' – i.e. understanding key concepts and texts within respective religious traditions (see Chapters 3, 4 and 6);*
(x) *developing understanding of, and formation within, a spiritual life (with particular reference to Chapter 6);*
(xi) *appreciating the relation between reason and faith and thus 'the reasonableness' of having and living a faith (see Chapters 3, 4 and 5).*

Introduction

This book attempts to address a problem in the battle for the soul of religious education, namely, that concerned with the reasonableness and thus the truth of religious belief.

An agreed tradition of religious faith, as a basis for understanding and for moral life, had been assured in the English and Welsh 1944 Education Act, as pointed out in Chapter 1, through 'religious instruction' and 'daily worship' (though retaining the right of withdrawal). Although such religious ethos was not explicitly stated to be Christian, it was generally assumed that it would be so.

However, as analysed in Chapter 1, many assumptions, which underpinned teaching of religious education a generation or so ago, no longer hold within a more secular society (as explained in Chapter 8) – namely, assumptions of Britain being in practice and ethos a Christian country, of the Christian story being essentially true, of broad agreement on moral living based on that Christian way of life, and of an expected duty of schools to support both the truth of those beliefs and the corresponding way of life reflected in daily assemblies, prayers and teaching of religious education. In particular, the basis for talking about the truth or 'reasonableness' of religious belief seems gradually to have disappeared together with any focus on a particular religious tradition.

The background to the arguments in this book, therefore, has been the undermining of the religious ethos due to the growing conviction that, since education is concerned with development of reason, and thus with the inherited claims to knowledge in its different forms, so religion, without seemingly a secure knowledge base, should not be taught as such. To repeat from Chapter I the argument of Professor Paul Hirst,

> There has already emerged in our society a view of education, a concept of education, which makes the whole idea of Christian education a kind of nonsense and the search for a Christian approach to, or philosophy of, education, a huge mistake.
>
> *(Hirst, 1965)*

Therefore, for example, the moral duties and virtues, as explained in Chapter 5, could no longer be bolstered by religious faith. The place of religious education was filled by different agendas concerned with personal and moral development, promoting social cohesion, or knowing *about* different religions and cultures, including humanism – as reflected in the 2017 Report of the Commission on Religious Education (see Chapter 1 of this book, pp. 13–14).

A complicating factor has been the establishment of different kinds of schools within the State system, reflecting either different or no religious affiliations: Community Schools, and Faith Schools, amongst which are to be distinguished Voluntary Controlled Schools (mainly Church of England, albeit embracing all within the respective catchment areas) and Voluntary Aided Schools (mainly, but not exclusively, Catholic), thereby ensuring, for those parents who wish it, a religious ethos and dimension in an otherwise increasingly secular system. The situation became more complicated with the advent of Academies, which are either in multi-academy chains outside of local authority responsibility or directly responsible to the Secretary of State. Undermined in such multiple-academies is often the close connection of Voluntary Aided schools with their parish, which, working with the parochial school, had a key role in the religious formation of the local children. Therefore, as David Fincham concluded in his paper, 'Hidden threat to gospel values':

> A critical question for Catholic academies when considering conversion to academy status is how far they can maintain their integrity, especially in their responsibility for the poor and powerless members of society.
> (*Tablet, 17.4.19*)

This, too, is becoming a problem in Ireland, where in an increasingly secularised society the close link between school and parish (for example, in preparation for First Communion and Confirmation) is in decline (see the Irish Times, 6.4.19, p. 15).

Such diversity in provision provokes *different challenges* to the place of religious identity in state-funded schools and to the nature of religious education which takes place within them. These challenges focus much upon questions concerning the 'reasonableness of having a faith' and thus of the beliefs and forms of life which the respective schools may wish to promote.

But challenges for religious education in non-religiously affiliated schools are understandably different from those which have an explicitly religious commitment. Therefore, in what follows, a distinction is drawn between the first seven challenges for religious education in schools without religious affiliation, and the added four challenges for schools with religious affiliation.

Challenges for religious education: schools without religious affiliation

First challenge: exploring the numinous, the 'mysterium tremendum' or the 'sacred' as outlined in Chapter 2

One may endeavour to evoke within the pupils what are elemental to all religious faiths, namely, those feelings of the 'mysterium tremendum', that sense of the 'numinous', as described in Chapter 2, and indeed thereby coming to recognise a possible spiritual side to their lives. One may see how for some this might be provoked through works of art, poetry or drama, religious artefacts, and stories, as pupils are encouraged to appreciate the feelings which underpin such experiences, and (with suitable help) to develop the spiritual sense, as described in Chapter 1, namely,

> the universal search for individual identity . . . the search for meaning and purpose in life and for the values by which to live'.
>
> *(NCC, 1993, p. 2)*

The 'spiritual' indicates a rising above the immediate and mundane. Otto's *The Idea of the Holy*, as seen in Chapter 2, quoted Wordsworth's *Tintern Abbey* as one such piece of spiritual appreciation. In this and other examples given, Otto (1923) speaks of the central religious idea of 'the holy' as something which can be

> evoked, awakened in the mind; as everything that 'comes of the spirit' must be awakened.
>
> *(p. 7)*

Such 'evocations' might be assisted by shared accounts between the lived experiences of young pupils, who are frequently bereft of religious appreciation in the secular world they inhabit. Jack Priestley pursued this in his 1985 paper, 'Towards finding the hidden curriculum: a consideration of the spiritual dimension of experience in curriculum planning'.

Such experiences have been explored by the Religious Experience Research Unit in the University of Oxford in the tradition of William James in, *The Varieties of Religious Experience* (see Chapter 2 of this book). Edward Robinson (1977), in his significantly entitled book, *The Original Vision, a Study of the Religious Experiences of Childhood*, includes children in that making of connections between everyday experiences and the intimations of religious awareness.

The purpose of early but crucial insight into religious consciousness (refusing to reduce religious education to 'mere knowledge', namely, facts and figures about different religions) would be to make links between that consciousness (as described by various authors in Chapter 2) and the students' own experiences. In so doing they may be encouraged to explore grounds for maintaining such beliefs and for living according to them. This is back to the phenomenological account of, and basis for, religious understanding, with special reference to Smart (1969, 1973) and described in Chapters 2 and 4. Scope would thereby be given to pupils' own inner experience, which too often is neglected in the 'transmission of knowledge'. As Priestley (1985) argued,

> The great purpose of education should be to give people greater reliance on the validity of their own inward and private experience, and thereby to 'understand religion' as one way of making sense of many inner experiences.

Such understanding would not *entail* 'belief', although it might lead on to seeing how belief in God might be considered 'reasonable'. As Gill and Thomson (2014, p. 6) suggest [and as explained in Chapter 6 of this book], there could be 'a continuum between thinner and thicker conceptions of the concept of the spiritual.

Second challenge: philosophical engagement with claims about the 'numinous' or the 'sacred'

Involved in this increasing awareness of responses to what people see as 'sacred' would be questions about the *reasonableness* of such awareness, requiring the *philosophical engagement* as argued for in Chapters 3 and 4. That subjective consciousness of the 'sacred' calls for examination of the claimed rational grounds for moving from subjective consciousness to the claimed truth of what would seem to be concluded. There are three aspects of this 'philosophical engagement' which are relevant to the development and delivery of religious education, but which create challenges for schools.

The first aspect relates to the notion of a 'Community of Inquiry', a term used by Matthew Lipman (2003) to change the environment within schools, which too often encourages acquisition of knowledge rather than freedom to think widely and openly within the community of the classroom. Especially is this the case with controversial issues of personal concern, of which religious beliefs and practices might be seen as prime examples. Such freedom of discussion on matters of importance would lie in clarification of meaning, identification of relevant evidence and openness to criticism from within the class community. In so doing, the discussants would enter into questions concerning moral significance of beliefs held, of practices engaged in (as shown in Chapter 5) and of the knowledge foundations for such beliefs and practices, as well as the validity of arguments made. They would be beginning to think philosophically, relating each person's contribution to statements and arguments made, rather than to the persons who made them. Such philosophical reflection and argument are habits to be acquired and in need of careful nurturing by teachers who themselves would refrain from imposing what they see to be the 'right answer', though doubtless raising questions at appropriate moments. In all this, Lipman indicates his indebtedness to the pragmatist philosophical thinking of John Dewey (1910), *How We Think*, where (p. 9) he lists 'the elements of reflective thinking':

> first, a state of perplexity, hesitation, doubt; and, second, an act of search or investigation directed at bringing to light further facts which serve to corroborate or to nullify the suggested belief.

The second aspect of 'philosophical engagement', relevant to the promotion of religious education, is the focus of such philosophical thinking on issues directly arising from religious beliefs. Questions of 'What do you mean?' would be addressed in regard to key concepts such as 'redemption', 'spiritual', 'worship', 'Torah', 'Shari'a' as they arise in the different accounts of religious belief or in accounts which pupils give of their religious practices. Hence, philosophy here aims at 'understanding', leading to greater insight, but always within a supportive (even if argumentative) community, conducted according to agreed rules of procedure. Moreover, such reflective exercises would encourage pupils to explore with each other aspects of everyday experiences which are in different ways meaningful, raising ethical questions about the life worth living or about the sense of mystery which some feel in their tentative experiences of the 'numinous' and which is intrinsic to an understanding of the divine. The teacher's role would be, not to direct towards previously decided conclusions, but rather to encourage exploration of ideas through mutual support.

A third aspect of 'philosophical engagement' would be that of raising issues concerning the truth or reasonableness of religious beliefs, drawing on different kinds of reason and evidence (such as summarised in Chapter 3), whereby faith has been justified as reasonable, although constantly open to critical discussion in the face of different degrees of doubt (as recognised in Chapter 6). Indeed, a challenge for religious education, whether in Faith Schools or schools without religious affiliation, would be to take seriously the doubts which may be held by pupils. In so doing, attention would need to be given to the distinctive role of philosophy in the clarification of beliefs, addressing critically, for example, the lasting influence of the Enlightenment and the dominance of science as the paradigm of knowledge and rationality (see, for example, Chapter 3, pp. 34–36). Relevant passages from key philosophers in this respect could be given for discussion. Thus, religious education might help pupils reflect critically on the truth and relevance of religious beliefs (Christian, Jewish, Islamic and other) and the extent to which that truth is relevant today, without requiring them to be committed to particular faiths and religious practices.

Third challenge: the sharing of what is common between, but also what differentiates, different faith traditions

Schools (whether Community, Voluntary Aided or Voluntary Controlled) have mixed populations of different religious affiliations and none. But much can be learnt from the different ways in which Christianity, Islam, Judaism and other religions have found means of articulating the spiritual experience of the numinous through their distinctive rituals, key texts, artistic creations, social relations and moral requirements. There is more in common than generally recognised. Each person, therefore, can be challenged and enlightened by coming to understand the rituals and requirements of other religious practices. This would recognise what is in common in their respective histories, philosophical enquiries, beliefs in God and moral traditions. Such recognitions would deepen understanding as well as promote mutual respect and a sense of shared community.

Return could profitably be made to the phenomenological approach to religious education (as seen in Chapter 1), the philosophical basis of which was explained in Chapter 4. Sharpe (1975) writes of the structuring of religious education around the 'horizons of meaning' of a range of religious traditions regarding their 'transcendent truth claims'. He argues,

> the phenomenological essence of religion is the intentionality of religious adherence, direction to the realm of the sacred and divine and transcendent by 'bracketing out' pupils' presuppositions (from a particular faith tradition) and particular world views.

Thus, as Grimmitt (1978), stated in his book, significantly entitled, *What can I do in RE?* (quoted in Copley, 1997, p. 112),

> Only when we can 'bracket out' ourselves, our preconceived notions and our particular values and concentrate on what, for example, a Muslim feels when he prays to Allah . . . will we begin to appreciate and understand the essence of Islam.

There are different religious languages but with common underlying claims, namely, that there is a Transcendent Being ultimately responsible for the phenomenal world in which we live and to whom we owe recognition through worship, prayer and a way of living. Each major religion, through ritual and art, attempts to capture, howsoever inadequately, that Transcendent Being. The curriculum opportunity to share and develop different perspectives on the same phenomenon (for example, through informed visits to the different places of worship) is one way in which resources from different faiths might illuminate the essence of religious experience and belief. As Marius Felderhof (2014, p. 17) asserts in Gill and Thomson's referred-to book,

> Why should one assume that a religiously plural society is incapable of agreeing on the kind of religious communications that would be acceptable to most religious communities? One obvious reason for potential agreement is that there are strong family resemblances amongst the various religious traditions; they have much in common. They invariably pray, contemplate and worship. . . . They encourage faith. They share key values.

Fourth challenge: moral dimension to life and formation of conscience

In raising matters of personal and social significance for systematic exploration and discussion, personal concerns are likely to arise in which the moral basis for conclusions reached could be challenged or seen to be in need of clarification. Back to Socrates' statement in Chapter 5, the 'unexamined life is not worth living'. The issues, which arise in pupils' raising personal and social questions, or in responding to those raised by others, give scope for deeper examination of the 'reasons why' of decisions made, or of actions proposed or of accounts of deeds done. Such discussions, rightly orchestrated, stimulate broader questions of morality and value at the personal, social and political levels. To these, as reflected in Chapter 5, the religious dimension and contribution would be difficult to dispense with even in a predominantly secular ambience. What makes someone distinctively human? What counts as human flourishing? The questions should be raised in the context of each person's ambitions and quandaries, and challenged by objections or supportive arguments.

Such group discussions and questioning, often beginning from consideration of specific incidents, requires identification of what seem to be relevant principles or (using Kant's word) 'maxims' as the basis for right action. These maxims can be challenged and thereby lead to more universalistic principles and to the sense of duty. For Kant, as explained in Chapter 5, the strong sense of obligation within such an informed conscience would demand the 'postulation' of a belief in the divine lawgiver. One cannot expect such an 'easy solution' in the weekly 'circle time' of schools, but those without religious belief could thus come to see the rationality of so having such belief. A philosopher of Kant's stature is not to be dismissed easily.

Fifth challenge: responding to a secular society

One way of understanding anything is to contrast it with something it is not. Here one would seek to see how religious forms of life contrast in various ways with the underlying values and beliefs of a society which has embraced very different 'horizons of significance' (to revert to Charles Taylor's words) in terms of personal well-being, social modes of behaviour and moral constraints (as argued in Chapter 8). Changes were reflected in the title of the Christmas course published by the Christian Education Movement in 1967: *The Secularisation of Society and the Role of the Christian Teacher*.

In such a secular environment religious education has attempted imaginative ways of relating closely to the issues and personal struggles concerning young people (summarised by Copley, 1997, pp. 66–88). Religious education cannot begin or continue as though there is a background of shared Christian values and understandings on which educational programmes might build – a set of teachings to be passed on. Hence, the significance of Harold Loukes' *Teenage Religion* (1961) which sought to 'personalise belief' through careful selection of texts and through discussion of them in relation to the problems and interests raised by the pupils. Loukes' syllabus was essentially 'problem-centred', namely,

> problems of personal relations: authority, friendship, sex and marriage and snobbery; problems of personal responsibility: money, work, leisure and prayer; problems of meaning: suffering, death and learning.
>
> (p. 71)

Hence, the significance, too, of Ronald Goldman, whose influential books, *Religious Thinking from Childhood to Adolescence* (1964) and *Readiness for Religion* (1965) emphasised religion, not so much as providing distinctive experience, but rather as reflecting on experience through the help of biblical stories and references.

Such changes in the 1960s in thinking and in practice were summed up by a commentator in the *Times Educational Supplement* (quoted in Copley, 1997, p. 81),

> Too often in the past we have tried to hand out theological answers before the children had the time to formulate the questions. In discussion based on life and experience the fundamental questions underlying the human condition become real. It then appears that religion in general, and Christianity in particular, are not so irrelevant as is often thought, and that committal to a way of life is obligatory for human existence.

Sixth challenge: finding the teachers

The final challenge for teaching religious education in schools without religious affiliation lies in finding enough suitably qualified teachers for such wide-ranging (and unpredictable) requirements for teaching such a subject, especially as it seems to have disconnected itself in many respects from a particular and shared religious tradition. The other subjects on the curriculum have agreed subject matter in terms of key concepts through which the subject matter is to be understood, criteria of truth and reasonableness, and inherited understandings of problems raised. But this seems no longer to be the case with religious studies (hence, the purpose of the present book). Therefore, it is not clear what counts as a specialist teacher in the subject. Teaching therefore so often depends on non-specialists.

Interim or 'half-way' conclusion

The preceding challenges are suggested as introductions to religious understanding, enabling pupils of whatever religious faith or none 'to enter into the conversation between the generations' on what have provided the 'horizons of significance' for most cultures and people. If a main purpose of education is to provide understanding of the personal and social worlds in which we live, then having a grasp of a religious form of life so widely shared is crucial. And this 'understanding' cannot be reduced simply to 'knowing about' other religions, or the superficial catalogue of facts about other cultures, which are sometimes recommended for religious education in our schools (see p. 9 in Chapter 1).

In gaining insight, pupils should be confronted with questions about the reasonableness of the beliefs, with the philosophical critiques which arise both within belief systems and from outside them, and with contrasts between religious ideals and current assumptions and values of the secular society they inhabit. Clearly such insight and deliberations have to be geared to the age of the pupils, and reference to 'communities of inquiry' (as explained in the philosophical challenge above) provides an example of the beginning (that is, the way of thinking and the need to respect different views) for that deeper reflection.

Challenges for religious education: schools with religious affiliation, Faith Schools

Such inclusive but changing understanding of religious education could not satisfy everyone. Monsignor Godfrey, the Catholic Apostolic Delegate, told Mr. Butler (Minister of Education, responsible for the 1944 Education Act and thereby for arrangements for religious education as a subject in all schools), that

> Catholics had no intention of selling the true concept of religion as the Anglicans had done.
>
> *(quoted in Copley, p. 25)*

Rather is having a faith a way of life, based on foundations which are claimed to be true, which transform how one sees the world and into which one needs to be initiated. Therefore, before we consider the further different challenges to such an understanding, it is necessary to point to issues arising from there being different kinds of Faith Schools.

The first issue is reflected in the distinction between Voluntary Controlled and Voluntary Aided schools. The former (largely Church of England) provide education, in terms of admissions and curriculum, for all within the local community irrespective of religious affiliation. Nonetheless, a series of reports by the Church of England (Dearing, 2001; Chadwick, 2012; Durham, 1970) argued for the importance of maintaining in the national educational system the values derived from the Christian inheritance, especially in view of the increasing domination

> by a secularist viewpoint indicative of an increasing utilitarian and materialist approach to education in which market economics would become the over-riding ethos of schools.
>
> *(Chadwick, 1997)*

Such schools, therefore, aim to provide an ethos derived from their religious foundations, and attach importance to religious education broadly conceived, no doubt meeting the challenges as outlined above. Such ethos emphasises the dignity and worth of each person, an ideal too easily undermined in the impersonal world of testing, league tables and competition.

Voluntary Aided schools, on the other hand, primarily Catholic, see religious education to be concerned more specifically with 'religious formation' and therefore complementary to the worshipping community of the parish. They set admissions criteria accordingly. However, in this more multi-cultural society, families of different religious cultures (especially Jewish and Muslim) also want schools which reflect their religious faiths. Furthermore, faith-based Voluntary Aided Schools frequently admit pupils not of that faith (over 25,000 Muslims attend Catholic schools). Different schools manage such a situation in different ways, some sharing what is common between them, having roots in their Abrahamic foundations and in the unfolding story of salvation, yet preserving opportunity for respective religious practices.

However, what follows in this section focuses on the challenges to religious education in the Catholic schools which constitute the vast majority of the Voluntary Aided. Following the restoration of the Catholic hierarchy in 1850, Cardinal Wiseman said the Catholic Church in England, serving especially the large influx of Irish people escaping the famine, should build parish schools before building their parish churches. There was seen to be an integration between schooling and parish life, both being concerned with the formation of people within a religious tradition in which human flourishing and fulfilment were to be understood.

Especially would this be true within an increasingly secular society, as explained in Chapter 8, which, through indifference to a religious way of defining what it means to be human or through different values or even through a degree of hostility, could undermine a religious form of understanding and way of life as these have developed. Just as immersion in a secular society helps form the way of thinking of the citizens of that society and of the educational aims which permeate its schools, so it is argued from within a religious tradition that those with distinctive ethical bases for human flourishing should be able to form their young people in a way which reflects their non-secular faith, provided of course that it meets public criteria for quality education (checked in the U.K. by the Inspectorate). This it would seek to do through specific practices (for example, its rituals and prayer life), theoretical understanding of those practices and distinctive spiritual ethos. Especially is that the case where such a religious tradition and its educational ideals have evolved over centuries through philosophical critique and theological scholarship, as argued in Chapters 2, 3 and 4.

Therefore, such schools have their own distinctive challenges for religious education, though starting with and building on the same challenges as those outlined above – in particular, the growing awareness of the 'numinous', the 'mysterium tremendum' and the 'sacred', but now as reflected in the liturgical year, life of prayer, and preparation for the sacramental life of the Eucharist and Confirmation. However, special room must also be made for those who feel and express doubts about their faith's underlying practices and rituals. Their growth here as elsewhere arises through doubt and criticism, as explained in Chapter 7.

Such challenges might be summarised as follows, but, first, recognising the difficulties described by Derek Lance, 1964, in the opening paragraph of his short book, *Till Christ be Formed*, (p. 13):

> Religion is irrelevant. This is the conviction of many today, and it is a view that is having an effect on our Catholic youth. To many Catholics the Church's message is not the Good News that will make sense of their lives, and the truth that will set them free. Rather, their faith, as they understand it, is a burden, a collection of dead doctrine, often couched in difficult, archaic language, which curbs and confines them.

The paragraph continues by arguing that 'they looked for an ideal and were given rules'.

Therefore, preservation of Faith Schools within the State system lies in the felt need to offer an alternative (*an ideal* of which Lance speaks) to the secular school and to the mind-set which is reflected in the prevailing influence of an increasingly secular society.

Seventh challenge: providing an ideal

That 'ideal', which, according to Lance, is what pupils so often looked for but failed to find, is to be found for the Christian, firstly, in the life, example and moral prescriptions of Jesus Christ in the Gospels, Epistles and Acts of the Apostles – the concern for the poor and sick, forgiveness of others for their misdeeds, opportunity for reparation of wrongs committed and instruction to 'love one another as I have loved you' – indeed, as summarised in the eleven Beatitudes of the Gospels and exemplified in such parables as that of the Prodigal Son.

However, it needs to be shown how such an ideal, exemplified in the life of Christ, can both reshape the lives of the pupils and offer hope where there may be despair. One might learn from the work of Loukes and Goldman, referred to above, how engagement of young people in discussions of their problems challenges prevailing social values which impact upon them, especially where reference is made to alternative understandings of human flourishing reflected in Christian texts and tradition. One could show ways in which Christians have bridged that divide between ideal and reality, providing inspiration to others. History is plentifully supplied with examples of men and women who have shown how the ideal, personified in Christ, can transform lives and communities, and create a sense of hope where there was despair. Part of such an ideal would be practical engagement in (as well as accounts of) efforts to help with problems of poverty, loneliness and sickness which prevail in the community.

But what is aimed at is more than consideration of the examples and recommendations of Christ and his followers but rather a recognition of how one's very identity is transformed by the 'internalising of Christ'. As St. Leo the Great exclaimed,

> Christian, recognise your dignity, and now that you have become a partaker of the divine nature, return not to the baseness of your former condition.
>
> *(see Lance, p. 18)*

Such a renewal of the religious consciousness and idealism is strongly argued for in the encyclical *Mater et Magistra:*

> We most earnestly beg the world over, all clergy and laity, to be deeply conscious of the dignity, the nobility, which is theirs through being grafted on

to Christ as shoots on a vine: 'I am the vine; you are the branches'. They are thus called to share in His own divine life; and since they are united in mind and spirit with the divine Redeemer even when they are engaged in the affairs of the world, their work becomes a continuation of His work, penetrated with a redemptive power.

Although such 'ideal' has referred specifically to Christian contexts, the same applies equally to other religiously affiliated schools such as the Jewish and Islamic. Indeed, where there are young people from different faiths in the class, a diversity of examples from different faiths would enrich understanding. But this can be only the beginning of a deeper understanding of the theological underpinnings of such ideals and of human dignity. Indeed, there is much in common between the different faiths, and, from the religious point of view, the differences should not be seen as a 'clash of civilisations' (as famously claimed by Huntingdon, 1996, in his book of that title). Indeed, in the recent visit to the United Arab Emirates, reflected in the document, *Human Fraternity for World Peace*, Pope Francis spoke of

> Muslims of the East and West, together with the Catholic Church and the Catholics of the East and West, declare the adoption of a cultural dialogue as the path; mutual cooperation as the code of conduct; reciprocal understanding as the method and standard.

There was recognition that different faiths belong to the same family and worship the same God. Similarly, the encyclical *Nostra Aetate*, the foundation document for Catholic relations with Jews and Muslims, refers to the one covenant between the Jewish people and Christians.

Eighth challenge: formation of social conscience

In the 'Fourth Challenge' (with reference in particular to Kant and Newman in the formation of conscience, as explained in Chapter 5), it was argued that essential to distinctively human development was the capacity and tendency to think through the consequences of one's choices and actions in terms of general principles of justification, and that such principles can, when challenged, be supported by more general accounts of what constitutes human flourishing, applicable to everyone. Such moral deliberation leads to recognition of one's duty – to the forming of conscience. As intimated earlier, such a questioning approach as to what one should do (either in hypothetical situations or in real life quandaries) gives rise eventually to very general principles of living and behaving in a morally sound manner within a just society. It might be called 'formation of social conscience' – a generalised sense spelt out in terms of 'common good', a leading document being that of the 1871 Encyclical *Rerum Novarum*. Therein lies the argument recognising the dignity of each member of society, irrespective of ethnic difference, with special reference to the poor and disadvantaged.

> First and foremost the Church offers its educational service to the poor or those who are deprived of family life and affection or those who are far from the faith.
> *(Sacred Congregation for Catholic Education, 1977)*

Religious education, to be true to a religious form of life, cannot dodge questions about the sort of society to be created which would reflect the ideals of a religious form of life.

Ninth challenge: religious literacy

Such deeper understanding requires a grasp of the concepts through which that distinctively Christian, Jewish or Muslim sense of human dignity and purpose might be understood and articulated. In that respect, religious understanding is like any form of knowledge, defined in terms of distinctive concepts and a distinctive way therefore of understanding reality. Just as, in learning physics, one needs to grasp such concepts as 'atom', 'neutron' or 'particle', so in religious understanding one needs to see experience through such concepts as 'holiness', 'grace', 'revelation', 'redemption', 'sacrament', 'Incarnation' – indeed, the very concept of 'God' as that is pursued in Chapters 3 and 4. One needs at the same time to recognise ways in which such reality might be understood on the basis, not of verification as that is pursued in the sciences, but of what constitutes appropriate evidence and reasonableness for claims made – again as developed in Chapters 3 and 4.

In many respects, such 'religious literacy' is covered in much detail in *Religious Education Curriculum Directory* (RECD) for Catholic schools, adapted so that religious education in such schools might remain acceptable as a subject for public examinations. But, as Sean Whittle (2019) argues, severe tension arises here between preserving RE as a respectable academic subject ('a knowledge heavy diet in RE ... ever increasing chunks of Catholic doctrine in all of their RE lessons') and seeing RE as the *formation* of children and students within a religious form of life, inspired by an ideal, as explained above, and developing a spiritual life, as explained below.

Tenth challenge: spiritual life and understanding

In the changing fortunes of religious education as revealed in Chapter 1, there remains constant reference to spiritual development. The 1944 Education Act stated its importance. But both there and in the several official statements and documents which followed, there was some confusion between a distinctively religious meaning, as in the DES/HMI document, *Curriculum 11–16.* (1977),

> everything in human knowledge or experience that is connected with or derives from a sense of God or of gods (ditto), and a more comprehensive

account, as in [the] 1993 National Curriculum Council (NCC) document, *Spiritual and Moral Development*, namely, the awareness which transcended ordinary everyday experience in terms of [an] underlying search for meaning in life arising from a sense of awe or of mystery.

One might say, of course, that the word 'spiritual', as indeed many words have different usages within a language, but in all its uses, as argued in Chapter 6, 'spiritual' would indicate an awareness which transcends the experience of the material world whether by pointing to a different order of explanation of events or by emphasising the dominance of certain feelings concerning the purpose or direction of one's life.

It takes on a more specific meaning within the context of religious understanding, where Gerald Grace, in his paper, 'The renewal of spiritual capital and the critique of the secular world' (2002a, p. 34), defines 'spiritual capital' as the

> resources of faith and values derived from commitment to a religious tradition,

particularly an awareness of, and engagement with, a moral form of life arising from religious beliefs,

> [resisting] external pressure for secularism, hedonism and materialism,

and promoting the intrinsic dignity (too often denied) of each person.

Or, again, Grace (2002b, p. 19) points to Durkheim's attempt in *The Elementary Forms of Religious Life* to define spirituality from the standpoint of religious sociology, namely,

> that which was sacred in a society [and] referred to things which were superior in dignity and power to the elements of mundane life, to things 'set apart', to notions of the transcendent and divine, of souls and of spirits and of the ultimate destiny of persons,

all of which take us back to the 'idea of the holy' or the 'reasons of the heart' as developed in Chapter 2, and as developed at greater length in Chapter 6.

The creation of such spirituality must be a further 'major challenge' for the school. Such an engagement would be encouraged within prayer and meditation, and in the 'imitation of Christ' and of his saints, but also in the explicit promotion of the sense of the 'common good', that profound respect for each individual irrespective of background. It would be explicitly contrasted with the materialism of the more secular society where, according to Grimmitt (1987, p. 120),

> traditional cultures of spirituality . . . are marginalised and silenced by the contemporary combination of bureaucracy, industry and the consciousness-creating media.

The challenge for religious education, therefore, is to ensure opportunities for informed recollection of the inner feelings, embodied in prayer and stimulated by appropriate examples and readings, with the opportunity to discuss and to reflect. All this would be aided by participation in liturgy, which manifests and encourages that spiritual perspective. This could be so conducted that even those of little faith might make connections with the broader, more inclusive sense of 'the spiritual', as described in Chapter 1, and as anticipated in the widespread occurrence of religious experience, broadly conceived, referred to in Chapter 2 (see Hay et al., 1996; and Priestley, 1985).

As Wright (1998, p. 29) succinctly puts it:

> If pupils were to learn 'from' rather than merely 'about' religion, then they must pass beyond the external manifestations of religious expression and enter into its experiential heart.

Eleventh challenge: philosophical reasonableness within a religious faith

Reference was made previously (in the second challenge) to Martin Lipman's *Philosophy for Children*, namely, the centrality in the philosophical discourse of carefully conducted discussion of controversial issues – controversial in the sense that there is disagreement about conclusions reached and about the ways in which such disagreement may be resolved.

Never could that be truer than in questions concerned with religious faith – and hence, with religious education. Progress requires clarification of key ideas and concepts, examination of appropriate evidence for (or mode of verification of) conclusions reached, and logical consequences of asserting specific conclusions. In all of these, one is taken into deeper philosophical territories of ethics, epistemology and philosophy of mind, as explained in Chapters 3 and 4. It was not without reason that, as explained in Chapter 2, Boethius' 5th-century book, *The Consolations of Philosophy,* referred to 'philosophy as the Lady Handmaiden of Theology'.

Such philosophical thinking, at whatever level (and, according to Lipman, that level can be developed in the child's early years) necessarily raises doubts in the learner's mind, but, as explained in Chapter 6, such doubting is inevitable in the growth of understanding. And, in philosophical debate, expressions of doubt should be encouraged and recognised as a spur to deeper and further understanding. If doubt is not treated sympathetically in such philosophical deliberations, it will remain unchallenged, smouldering away until finally released into the secular world.

Bibliography

Chadwick, P., 1997, *Shifting Alliances: Church and State in English Education*, London: Cassell.
Chadwick Report, 2012, *Going for Growth: Transformation for Children, Young Persons and the Church*, London: SPCK.
Congregation for Catholic Education, 1977, *The Catholic School*, Vatican.

Copley, T., 1997, *Teaching Religion*, University of Exeter Press.
Dearing Report, 2001, *Way Ahead: Church of England Schools in the New Millennium*, London: Church House Publications.
DES/HMI, 1977, *Curriculum*, vols. 11–16, London: DES.
Dewey, J., 1910/1997, *How We Think*, New York: Dover Publications.
Durham Report, 1970, *The Fourth R: The Report of the Commission on Religious Education in Schools*, London: SPCK.
Felderhof, M.C., 2014, *Educating Persons: The Role of Religious Education*, in Gill, S. and Thomson, G., *Redefining Religious Education*, London: Palgrave MacMillan.
Fincham, D., 2019, 'Hidden threat to gospel values', *Tablet*, 17 April 2019.
Goldman, R., 1964, *Religious Thinking from Childhood to Adolescence*, Routledge and Kegan Paul.
Grace, G., 2002a, 'The renewal of spiritual capital and the critique of the secular world', in Grace, G., ed., *Catholic Schools: Mission, Markets and Morality*, London: Routledge.
Grace, G., 2002b., 'The sacred and the secular', in Grace, G., ed., *Catholic Schools: Mission, Markets and Morality*, London: Routledge.
Grimmitt, M., 1987, *Religious Education and Human Development*, Great Wakering, Essex.
Hay, D., Nye, R., and Murphy, R., 1996, 'Thinking about Childhood Spirituality: Review of research and current directions', in Francis, L.J. et al., eds., *Research in Religious Education*, Leominster: Gracewing.
Hirst, P.H., 1965, 'Morals, Religion and the Maintained School', in *British Journal of Educational Studies*, 14.
Huntingdon, S.P., 1996, *The Clash of Civilisations: The Remaking of the World Order*, New York: Simon and Shuster.
James, W., 1902, *Varieties of Religious Experience*, London: Gifford Lectures.
Lance, D., 1964, *Till Christ Be Formed: Teaching Religion as the History of Salvation*, London: Darton, Longman and Todd.
Lipman, M., 2003, *Thinking in Education*, Cambridge University Press.
Loukes, H., 1961, *Teenage Religion*, SCM Press.
Loukes, H., 1973, *Teenage Morality*, SCM Press.
NCC (National Curriculum Council,1993) *Spiritual and Moral Development*, London: DES.
Otto, R., 1923/1958, *The Idea of the Holy*, Oxford: Oxford University Press.
Pew Centre for Research, 2012, Washington, DC.
Priestley, J., 1981, 'Religious story and the literary imagination', *British Journal of Religious Education*, 4(1).
Priestley, J., 1985, 'Towards finding the hidden curriculum: a consideration of the spiritual dimension of experience in curriculum planning', *British Journal of Religious Education*, 7 (3).
Pring, R., 2019, *Thinking Philosophically About Education*, London: Routledge.
Robinson, E., 1977, *The Original Vision, a Study of the Religious Experiences of Childhood*, Oxford: Manchester College.
Sacks, J., 1997, *The Politics of Hope*, London: Jonathan Cape.
Sharpe, E.J., 1975, 'The phenomenology of religion', *Learning for Living*, 15 (1).
Smart, N., 1969, *The Religious Experience of Mankind*, London: Palgrave Macmillan.
Smart, N., 1973, *The Phenomenon of Religion*, London: Palgrave Macmillan.
Swan Report, 1985, *Education of Children from Ethnic Minority Groups*, London: HMSO.
Whittle, S., 2019, 'Take care – changes are on the horizon for RE in Catholic schools', *Networking*, 20 (2).
Wright, A., 1998, *Spiritual Pedagogy*, Abingdon: Culham College Institute.

10
INDOCTRINATION?

This final chapter addresses the accusation of indoctrination frequently directed at those who seek to teach religious studies and thereby initiate their pupils into a religious form of life. But such an accusation ignores the long tradition of philosophical and spiritual thinking which justifies the reasonableness of religious belief, and thus the connection between faith and reason. Therefore, one might well ask: who is doing the indoctrinating?

In the light of this book's account of what counts as 'reasonableness' in having and developing religious knowledge, and thereby in supporting a religious form of life, must such a religious education be open to accusation of 'indoctrination', as so often stated? This indeed has become an assumption in the criticism of religious education in schools. We need therefore to consider carefully what such an accusation means. Is Dawkins (2011) correct to assert, not on empirical evidence, but with strong conviction that

> the most obvious and serious case of government-imposed religion [does not] so much teach about religion as indoctrinate in the particular religion that runs the school?
>
> (*New Statesman,* 19.12.11)

Clearly it is necessary to think more clearly about what we mean by indoctrination before we know who is doing the indoctrinating.

Indoctrination would imply that a person

- has been taught certain beliefs (especially those which are controversial) without there being appropriate evidence for those beliefs,

- in such a way that the believer has no doubts about their truth, despite the claimed lack of evidence,
- such that the believer cannot then dispense with what are seen to be basic and unquestioned beliefs, whatever the contrary arguments and evidence.

Hence, teaching religion as a form of knowledge, and thereby the development of 'religious formation', would be seen, by definition, as a form of indoctrination. The so-called 'knowledge' is seen to lack verification, even in principle. Thus John White (1967), in his detailed analysis of the meaning of indoctrination, argued that the teaching of Roman Catholicism must be indoctrination because they are teaching as true what cannot be demonstrated as true.

> Therefore, many of them [the teachers] are fully prepared to accept rational discussion of these doctrines in their teaching, for they do not believe that such discussion could ever undermine them
>
> (p. 182)

In response, it has been argued in this book that, though lacking the sort of verification which characterises empirical knowledge, religious beliefs can be *reasonable*, based as they are on long and critical traditions in making sense of experience of different kinds. Such critical traditions arise from doubts which need to be (and have constantly been) addressed in the light of further evidence and argument. Such reasonableness may not entail absolute certainty, as indeed such certainty escapes even scientific claims to knowledge where such knowledge grows through criticism of what previously was accepted as true. There is a need therefore to distinguish verification (in the strict and empirical sense) from belief held on 'appropriate evidence' (as in political and social sciences) which opens up a much wider range of reasonable beliefs, as in the evaluation of the arts, in moral deliberations, and in political and social studies. Initiation into such beliefs makes possible an informed critique of them, in which doubt (as described in Chapter 6) is acceptable, and thereby the further development of understanding.

As Callan (2009) wrote in defence of 'initiation', so often seen as the mark of indoctrination by the anti-religious lobby,

> The initiation of children into religious practice could secure an understanding of religion unavailable, or at least less available, in the absence of initiation, and the relevant understanding enables or enhances in some way an autonomous choice regarding religion.

Indeed, such an initiation seems more and more necessary in order to counterbalance the overwhelming influence of the secular society which the young people inhabit. If initiation implies 'indoctrination', then those who have never been initiated into a religious view of things might similarly be accused of being indoctrinated with regard to their belief in the unreasonableness of religious beliefs.

Bibliography

Callan, E., 2009, 'Why bring the kids into this?' in Haydon, G., ed., *Faith in Education: A Tribute to Tony McLoughlin*, London: IoE.

Dawkins, R., 2011, 'The Tyranny of the Discontinuous Mind,' *New Statesman*, Dec. 19, 2011.

White, J., 1967, 'Indoctrination', in Peters, R.S., ed., *The Concept of Education*, London: RKP.

NAME INDEX

Al-Farabi 41
Al-Gazzali, A. H. 41
Anselm, St. 21, 53, 75, 79, 82
Aquinas, T. 3, 4, 7, 22, 30, 36, 42, 45, 46, 49, 53, 80, 82
Aristotle 29, 41–43, 50, 60
Arnold, M. 92–93
Augustine, St. 45, 49, 54, 67, 71, 82, 83
Averroes 41, 45
Avicenna 41, 42, 45
Ayer, A. J. 34, 39, 46, 36, 60, 61, 81

Babbage, C. 38
Bach, J.S. 12
Berkeley, Bishop 79
Boethius 21, 27, 54, 78, 116
Bonaventure, St. 1, 82
Boyle, R. 38
Brentano, F. 39, 40
Brieskorm, E. 99
Briggs, A. 38
Brown, C. 10
Burbage, R. 3

Callan, E. 119
Carlyle, T. 25–28
Carr, D. 12, 13
Chadwick, P. 8, 110
Chardin, T. 44
Cooling, T. 34
Copleston F. 5, 7, 67, 83
Copley, T. 8, 10, 107, 108, 109, 110
Copson, A. 14
Cottingham, J. 24, 28, 84, 85, 92

Dawkins, R. 23, 37, 80, 118
Descartes, R. 2, 26, 56, 78–80, 92
Dewey, J. 105
Dostoevski, F. 64
Durkheim, E. 2, 26, 89–90, 94, 98

Eliot, T.S. 47, 84
Elliott, G. 3

Farrer, A. 53, 54
Felderhof, M. 107
Fincham, D. 103
Four Arrows 73
Francis, Pope 113
Francis of Assisi, St. 55

Gearon, L. 6, 8, 9, 39
Gill, S. 13, 70, 73, 105
Gilson, E. 43, 44, 50
Goldman, R. 108–109, 112
Grace, G. 9, 27, 115
Grimmitt, M. 107, 115
Guizot, F. 94
Gurney, P. 3

Habermas, J. 92, 94, 96, 98–99
Halstead, M. 8
Halvorson, H. 38
Harlen, N. 37
Harries, R. 49, 53, 60, 84
Harris, S. 37
Hay, D. 116
Hebblethwaite, P. 82
Heidegger, M. 40

Name index

Hesse, H. 60
Hewer, C.T.R. 23
Hilliard, E.W. 8
Hirst, P.H. 4, 102
Hitchins, C. 37
Hobbes, T. 66
Holm, J. 10
Hopkins, G.M. 25
Huberry, D.S. 33
Hume, D. 3, 5, 37, 60, 61
Husserl, E. 10, 40

Ignatius of Loyola, St. 74–75

Jackson, R. 11, 16
James, W. 20, 23, 27–30, 39, 41, 76, 104
John of Damascus 49

Kant, E. 36, 40, 41, 50, 61–63, 67, 68, 99, 108
Kenny, A. 23, 29, 38, 80, 81, 88
Kepler, J. 38, 43
Kierkegaard, S. 20
Knox, R. 79

Lance, D. 111–112
Leibniz, G.W. 43
Lennox, J. 38, 43
Leo XIII, Pope 65, 94, 112
Locke, J. 37, 93
Lipman, M. 105, 116
Lonergan, B. 24
Loukes, H. 108, 112
Lyotard, J-F. 35

MacIntyre, D. 42
MacMurray, J. 9
Maimonides 42
Maitland, O. 3, 4, 17
Martin, Archbishop 15
Maxwell, C. 38
McGrath, A. 83–84
Mendel, G. 38
Michelangelo 50
Miller, J. 7
Mohammad 20, 21, 23
More, T. 94
Mountford, B. 73

Nasr, S.H. 72–73
Neitzsche, F. 88–89, 91–92, 94, 95

Newman, J.H. 21, 30, 38, 45–47, 63–64, 67, 82, 91

Oakeshott, M. 59
O'Connell, S. 15
Otto, R. 20, 24–30, 39, 46, 76, 104

Pascal, E. 20, 24–30, 38, 39, 41, 46, 71, 76, 86
Pasteur, L. 38
Paul, St. 65
Platinga, A. 29, 83
Plato 27, 56, 60
Popper, K. 37, 38, 45, 77
Priestley, J. 10, 11, 27, 104–105, 116
Pring, R. 1, 52, 90

Ratzinger, J. (Pope Benedict) 92, 94, 96–99
Rees, M. 44
Robinson, E. 27, 104
Ruskin, J. 24

Sacks, J. 22, 66
Sartre, J-P. 64
Schuller, F. 94
Sharpe, E.J. 106–107
Sheldrake, P. 70–71
Smart, N. 11, 12, 40, 104
Socrates 56, 60, 73
Steane, A.J. 38
Stern, J. 37
Strom, M.S. 58
Swinburne, R. 29, 43, 64, 84, 86

Taylor, C. 3, 8, 81–82, 89, 90, 92, 93, 95–96, 108
Temple, Archbishop 5
Teresa of Avila 55
Thomas a Kempis, T. 47, 75
Thomson, G. 13, 70, 73, 105

Ward, K. 49, 50, 56
White, J. 119
Wilkinson, M. 9, 11, 42, 55
Wintersgill, E. 17
Wiseman, Cardinal 111
Wittgenstein, L. 42, 43
Wittle, S. 114
Wordsworth, W. 24, 25, 70, 104
Wright, A. 7, 13, 17, 33, 116

Young, M.F.D. 36

SUBJECT INDEX

aesthetic experience 12, 70
arts 10, 40, 104

belief 33–47; assent, real and notional 45, 46, 47
Bristol Agreed Syllabus 16
BSA, 2018, *British Social Attitudes Survey* 7, 8, 91

Catholic Church schools 5, 6
Catholic Education Council 4, 111
certainty 45, 77–78
Chadwick Report 8, 110
Christian, culture, inheritance and education 1, 3, 4, 8, 74–75, 102, 112
Church of England 5, 7, 103, 110
Commission on Religious Education 1, 103
community cohesion 9
community of inquiry 105
conscience clause 4
conscience, formation of 60–64, 107, 113–114
Cowper-Temple clause 4
CRE, 2017 (Commission on Religious Education) 1, 3, 16, 10

Dearing Report 1, 8, 110
DES/HMI Curriculum 11–16, 114
doubt: coping with 77–86; degrees of 80–81
Durham Report 8, 110

education: aims 4; system 2
Education Acts: 1870 4; 1944 5, 6, 102; 1988 6
Enlightenment 25, 27, 33, 36, 45, 71, 92
ethnic minorities 9
evil, problem of 82–85

faith: meaning 20–31; traditions 106–107; way of life 29–30
Faith Schools 1, 2, 4, 13, 15, 34, 103, 106, 110–112

God: belief in 33–47; existence of: nature of (through design, analogy, revelation, spiritual tradition) 49–56; proof, efficient, final causality 41–46

holy, idea of 25–28, 46, 104
horizons of significance 3, 109
human flourishing/development 58–60, 111
humanist perspective 3, 14, 93–95

indoctrination 2, 7, 8, 16, 22, 118–120
Ireland 1, 2, 3, 7, 15, 103
Islam, philosophy and practice 9, 10, 21, 23, 41, 42, 45, 72–73, 113

Judaism: Board of Deputies of British Jews 14; philosophy and practice (Torah) 20, 22, 23, 42, 113

Subject index

knowledge, truth, proof, evidence 9, 16–18, 20, 33–36, 39–46

literature 10

modernity 36–39
moral dimension 58–68; moral reasoning, deliberation, consciousness 91–92; religious forms of life 64–67; values and virtues 60–63
multi-cultural society 2, 9
music 10, 12, 25, 26, 40
Muslim *see* Islam
'mysterium tremendum' 49, 103, 111

National Association of Teachers of Religion 7
NCC (National Curriculum Council) 12, 14, 21, 69
Non-conformists 1, 5
North American indigenous people 73–74
numinous 23, 25, 103, 104, 105, 111

Ofsted 9, 14

parents 2, 4
person, nature of 96–97
Pew Research Center 9
phenomenological understanding 10–12, 39–41, 104, 107
philosophy/philosophical thinking 1, 2, 33, 105–106, 116
poetry 104
post-modernism 35

QCA, 2004 (Qualifications and Curriculum Authority) 11

rational/reasonableness 27–29, 33, 39, 42, 71, 105–106, 119
reason and faith 1, 2, 16–18
REDCo (Religious Education Council for England and Wales) 13–14
religious belief: assent 46–47; rational foundation 2, 3, 4, 9, 11, 33–36, 39–46; way of life 47, 70
religious education: challenges 70, 101–116; changing conceptions 3, 5–13; curriculum 1, 4, 114; ethos 2, 102; experience 104; formation/initiation 2, 5, 6, 70; scripture/bible 5–6
Religious Experience Research Unit 104

SACRE 6
sacred 40, 103, 105, 111
schools, organisation: academies 103; common school 6; Voluntary Aided 6, 103; Voluntary Controlled 6, 103, 110
Schools Council 7
secular: culture/context 1, 3, 88–99; education (system of) 2, 94; Secular League 4; society 1, 5, 7, 16, 89–90, 108–109
social cohesion 9
Spens Report 5, 6, 21
spiritual tradition 9, 12–13, 69–76, 104, 114–116
Swann Report 9, 16

teachers 109
theology 70–71
Toledo Guiding Principles 9
Transcendent Being 22–25, 71, 107

world views 1, 3, 14

For Product Safety Concerns and Information please contact our EU
representative GPSR@taylorandfrancis.com
Taylor & Francis Verlag GmbH, Kaufingerstraße 24, 80331 München, Germany

www.ingramcontent.com/pod-product-compliance
Lightning Source LLC
Chambersburg PA
CBHW070627300426
44113CB00010B/1687